LIGHTEN UP BUT TIGHTEN UP

A Fresh Sabbath Journey Quest

Sam Hunter

HIGH BRIDGE BOOKS

This book is dedicated to Irv Philpot, who started and accompanied me through this Sabbath exploration and journey. With seven very active children, he faced much greater resistance and suffered much more than I as he stayed true to his commitment to honor his Heavenly Father by honoring His day.

CONTENTS

A MESSAGE FROM A MOTHER

Why Your Children Need the Sabbath
by Jen Wilkin
Provided by THEGOSPELCOALITION
Used with permission

M Y OLDEST SON STARTED HIGH SCHOOL THIS FALL. AT
his orientation, the counselors spoke to parents about the
greatest challenge they see students face in school.

I expected to hear about poor study habits or substance abuse,
but to my initial surprise, these were not at the top of the list. Apparently, the greatest challenge presenting itself in the office of the
high school guidance counselor is a growing number of kids struggling with anxiety and depression.

Can you guess why?

A combination of overscheduling and sleep deprivation, linked
to two main contributors: electronics use and extracurricular activities. We were encouraged as parents to go home and talk to our teenagers about setting boundaries in these areas. Parents across the
auditorium scribbled notes furiously as the counselors outlined
some suggestions: limit texting, monitor bedtimes, cut back on team
practices. I couldn't help but think to myself: *Tonight there will be
many demonstrations of teenage angst when Mom shows up with her new
list of suggestions.*

What is unfolding at my son's high school is a clear illustration
of spiritual truth: the need for regular periods of rest in our lives.

From the earliest pages of the Bible, we find God instituting patterns of activity and rest — not just any kind of rest, but rest with the intent to engage in worship and community. The concept of Sabbath weaves its way through the Old Testament and the New, occupying a prominent place among the Ten Commandments and informing our understanding of heaven.

Despite biblical precedent, few Christians understand or practice Sabbath as a regular part of life, and, consequently, neither do their children.

Christian parents bear the responsibility of teaching our children the value of rest, through our words and through our actions. Children don't set the calendar in our homes — if they are over-scheduled or sleep deprived, the fault lies with us. How can we better discharge our duty of raising children to seek Sabbath? To value downtime to reconnect with God and family?

While I admire the high school guidance counselors' optimism, age 14 is probably too late to start imposing boundaries on our child's rest habits and schedule. We need a plan, and we need it early. How will we safeguard for our families the key Sabbath concepts of rest, worship and community?

(The remainder of this article is in Appendix A.)

WHAT COMPELLED ME TO WRITE THIS BOOK

NOTE: *I wrote this ten years ago, (2013) before I met my wife, Dina. I have edited and updated this, of course, but I chose not to change the setting nor the timing. Yet rest assured Dina has enthusiastically embraced this honoring of the Sabbath along with me, and she is a safeguard against us, "Doing as you please on God's holy day." (Isaiah 58:13)*

A YEAR AGO I WAS IN NEW YORK LISTENING TO EUGENE Peterson, author of The Message, talk about how much keeping the Sabbath has transformed his life. He went so far as to say it has transformed his preaching, his understanding of God's Word and his purpose, and his marriage and yes, even his health – mental and physical.

I remember sitting there listening to Eugene, thinking to myself, "What is he talking about? "Keeping the Sabbath ...," who even calls it the Sabbath anymore? No one I think I would want to hang out with would."

Eugene kept smiling, with his winsome way, as he talked about his and his wife's exploration of the Sabbath. It was almost as if he was recounting a wonderful vacation or a happy time earlier in their lives. His enthusiasm was compelling, and I couldn't help but be intrigued.

But I was still baffled. I could see his enthusiasm for the Sabbath, and I was sensing his encouragement, but keeping the Sabbath? Wasn't this kind of old school ... sort of Old Testament living? The only man I knew who truly kept the Sabbath was my pastor friend Det Bowers. No doubt there were others; I just didn't know any.

We have a university in my hometown of Greenville, S.C., Bob Jones University. A world-renowned Christian university. BJU is also renowned for being what many would call extreme fundamentalists. I'm thinking they probably observe the Sabbath out there, but who wants to be like them? So old-fashioned, so not with it.

A few months later I'm in California listening to Rob Bell talk about his newfound affection for the Sabbath. He was recently retired from the pulpit, and for the first time had no formal Sunday responsibilities. Again, I listened intently to Rob's energetic storytelling about his family's Sabbath adventure.

Rob Bell would never be mistaken for conservative fundamentalism, nor might Eugene Peterson. So I was running out of excuses.

It was abundantly clear that both these men, from very different backgrounds, as well as very different approaches to ministry, were on identical tracts surrounding the joy and glory, and the holiness, of keeping the Sabbath as God intended.

As obvious as their excitement and enthusiasm was, not to mention their reverent awe for the Lord, and his 4th Commandment to keep the Sabbath holy, I was still stuck with the idea, "Okay, this is good for them, they're a lot holier that I, and are obviously more sold-out for the Lord.

"But this doesn't, or ... *cannot* ... apply to me. Not living in the modern, real world."

Or so I thought. Looking back on my immature and uninformed mindset, and Eugene's and Rob's passionate stories, I see how totally blind I was to the Sabbath, how much I was missing it, as well as my understanding of God's heart behind the Sabbath.

And then a few months ago, during a men's gathering in which I was leading a panel discussion, I asked this question to my three panelist friends: "What one thing stands out in your mind that has propelled you deeper into the Kingdom, brought you closer to God, and opened up his loving plan for your life?"

A good question, don't you think? I'm pretty smart, at times.

It was my pastor friend Det's answer that stopped me in my tracks:

"Keeping the Sabbath holy," Det said quickly and unequivocally.

Uh oh. Here was that Sabbath thing again. I couldn't escape it!

Okay, now I'm no spiritual giant, but even I could see God was driving home a point to me:

"Do you get it, Sam? I want you to learn about, live out, and teach about my sacred Sabbath."

I got it – "Message received loud and clear, Father."

But as I pondered this idea of "keeping the Sabbath" I experienced a growing uneasiness and a troubling awareness of just how much I – we – *you*? have completely and totally ignored this commandment from God.

Oh, come on, isn't it true? You don't have a clue about the Sabbath. You're likely already thinking this is an exercise in futility. If you live in the South, the Sabbath is not the *Sabbath*, it's Sunday. And on Sunday we go to church, and many even to Sunday School. We have a nice midday meal (in the South it's called Sunday dinner) and then the rest of the day is ... ours.

But to keep it holy? What does that mean? And what would that look like? Certainly no fun, that's for sure.

You are just like I was, totally missing it. Totally blind to this gift from God. I'm no spiritual giant; I just had my eyes opened to the Sabbath, and like the blind man in John Chapter 9, even though I may be missing some of the deeper theology of the Sabbath, I now know "I was blind, but now I see."

So can you, if you will stick with me through this. Out of courtesy I have kept this to a manageable length. In all my writings I try to be succinct and to the point. That's my end of the bargain. Yours is to appreciate this efficiency and read through to the end.

There is a new life out there for you. God wants it for you. You can have it. But not until you start to live out his intentions for the Sabbath.

Let's go after it together!

WHY "LIGHTEN UP BUT TIGHTEN UP?

Because this was Jesus' consistent message to the uptight legalists:

> When Jesus had finished speaking, a Pharisee invited him to eat with him; so he went in and reclined at the table. 38 But the Pharisee was surprised when he noticed that Jesus did not first wash before the meal.
>
> 39 Then the Lord said to him, "Now then, you Pharisees clean the outside of the cup and dish, but inside you are full of greed and wickedness. 40 You foolish people! Did not the one who made the outside make the inside also? 41 But now as for what is inside you—be generous to the poor, and everything will be clean for you.
>
> 42 "Woe to you Pharisees, because you give God a tenth of your mint, rue and all other kinds of garden herbs, but you neglect justice and the love of God. You should have practiced the latter without leaving the former undone. (Luke 11:37-42)

In essence: You are too tight in your legalist performance, and way too light where it counts: Your hearts.

You see, I can feel good about myself if I technically perform well, but Jesus is asking me to look into my heart, to be aware of the darkness lurking within. His Lighten Up – Tighten Up message penetrates throughout our lives, not just on Sabbaths.

We have tightened up our performance so no one can criticize our behavior, but we are way too loosy-goosy in our hearts, where it counts the most, allowing a vast variety of negative thoughts and emotions, sinful and sloppy.

1

A GIFT?

The savings bank of human existence is the weekly Sabbath.

—William Garden Blaikie

D ID YOU KNOW THE SABBATH COMMANDMENT IS ONE of the most repeated commandments in all of the Holy Scriptures – by far? And just a cursory study will show how overwhelmed the Jews were by this directive from God. But being overwhelmed by the magnitude of this commandment led the Israelites to a legalistic obsession with it.

Our approach in this book is to glean the positive: overwhelmed by the importance of – but to sidestep the legalistic obsession.

It is one of the most repeated commandments, so it must be important to God. And therefore, as with all your loving Heavenly Father's commandments, it must be important *for* us.

A valuable lesson I've learned after walking with God for these past eighteen years is just that: whatever is important *to* him is only important to him because he knows how important it is *for* us. God doesn't dispense rules for the sake of rules. He has no interest in issuing commandants just to see if we will follow them, and punish us if we don't.

Your Heavenly Father is no assistant principal in the sky, in charge of discipline and wandering the school halls hoping to catch someone and punish them, just for the power trip. God has no ego. He simply loves you. He wants the best for you.

Yes, he always wants the best for you. As a matter of fact, as the Apostle Paul exclaims, he wants "immeasurably, abundantly more than anything you could ask for, or even imagine, in your wildest dreams to ask for." (Ephesians 3:20 paraphrase)

Let's stop for a moment and examine this idea first. Do you believe it? Do you trust in the fact God wants immeasurably, abundantly more than anything you could ask for, or even imagine, in your wildest dreams to ask for? I doubt you do. You might say you do, but in your heart of hearts?

A.W. Tozier observed that the most important thing about you is what comes to your mind when you think of God. Now that's a bold statement, but one I believe to have merit. If it is indeed true, then why is it? Why would the most important thing about you be what you think about God?

PROTECT NOT PROHIBIT

> *I am saying this for your own good, not to restrict you, but that you may live in a right way in undivided devotion to the Lord.*

> —1 Corinthians 7:35

If, when you think of God, you think of a loving Father who wants only the best for you, always and only, and all the time, it stands to reason you would view his commandments as positive guidelines for "the life that is truly life." Not pedantic rules, but loving and protecting prescriptions for both staying away from trouble and finding the A+ life.

However, if you think of God as that assistant principal, determined to be sure nobody's having any fun, you'll view his commandments in the same, negative, light. You will think his commandments are rules to prohibit you from having your way, not protect you from a C- life.

As Dallas Willard puts it:

> In the same way, we demean God immeasurably by casting him in the role of the cosmic boss, foreman or autocrat, whose chief joy in relation to humans is ordering them around, taking pleasure in seeing them jump at his command and painstakingly noting down any failures. (Hearing God)

Or, perhaps you view God as *necessary*, but not pertinent. Oh sure, you know there is a God, and you've been told all your life he is a loving God, but in your mind, the reality is that God is not relevant for your world.

He is necessary in the sense you know not to ignore him, not totally anyway. That's what Sundays (not Sabbaths) are for, right? So you give him his due. And what is his due? Oh, about two hours on Sunday morning. That, and a prayer before meals, only at home of course, and only sometimes.

Now to be sure you don't want to get in trouble with him, but when it comes to the details of your busy, and modern life, God is more like a taxi driver, waiting to give you a ride when you're in trouble, or have a pressing need.

But not so much for the details of running your life.

That is a prescription for the C- life. And I see it all around me.

Is that you?

I believe God wants only the best for me, and his commandments are for this very purpose. Yes, I absolutely believe this. But when it came to the Sabbath, I was still fuzzy on how keeping the Sabbath holy could apply to my life.

Okay, so I going to try to obey God in this commandment. So what? How will this possibly affect my life? I just do not see the importance.

But I was about to find out.

Again, since the Sabbath Commandment is one of the most repeated commandments in all of the Holy Scriptures – by far - it must be important to God. So it must be important *for* us. So let's keep going.

TWELVE WEEKS

It was obvious to me this commandment is the most ignored commandment of all. And not just ignored, but violated, trampled upon, and completely disrespected. I began to notice no one around me was observing the Sabbath, keeping it holy. No one! And don't tell me you are the exception, because you're not.

The more I pondered this commandment, and what I had heard from Eugene and Rob and Det, as well as Jesus, of course, the more obvious it became that we are all missing a huge gift.

But I had no clue what to do about it.

How does one keep the Sabbath holy? Am I to go back to the Dark Ages? Do I need to live on a farm, or become a monk? I had no application for keeping the Sabbath, other than doing nothing … fun.

Rob Bell gave us some very good advice while I was in California: "Before teaching on anything, live it out for a few weeks or even a few months."

So I did. I spent 12 weeks seeking to keep the Sabbath holy before teaching on it, and what an adventure it became! As we journey together through this book, I plan to share with you from time to time my weekly Sabbath Log: lessons I learned, ideas I discovered, and things God made clear to me: "Yes, Sam, that is in harmony with my Sabbath." "No, that idea, that activity, is not."

BABY STEPS

Where to begin?

At the beginning, with God's heart ... his intention behind this commandment. I know you'd like to just skip directly to the, "Give me a list. What can I do, and what can I not do on the Sabbath?" - and we will explore those questions later. But if we take that route first we are following the Pharisees into legalism.

Jesus never taught *about* the Sabbath, with a list of dos and don'ts. He certainly never handed out a list. But as he promised in the Sermon on the Mount, he lived it out ... he fulfilled it:

> "Do not think that I have come to abolish the Law or the
> Prophets; I have not come to abolish them but to fulfill
> them." (Matthew 5:17)

Don't miss that: Jesus did not teach about the Sabbath. He did not give lectures on "How to and how not to: Rules for successful Sabbath living." Instead of bringing us yet another list of dos and don'ts, he showed us the Sabbath is about our hearts.

Which takes us back to God's heart.

Is God for you? Is he about protecting you or prohibiting you? Is everything he asks and commands you to do good news? Yes, he is indeed for you, and yes, he is always about protecting you, and yes, his commandments are always good news. Even when they might not appear to be.

Let's pause and do a little exercise I did with the men at this early stage of our Sabbath Journey:

Let's say you love to play golf on Sunday – or fish – or watch NFL games – or work in the yard – or whatever, you get the picture. What if the Lord asks you not to do that anymore on the Sabbath? Okay, calm down. I'm not saying he will. I'm just asking what if he did?

Here at the beginning of your journey, before we fully explore God's heart and his gift of the Sabbath, is there any way you could say this would be good news? If he asked you to stop, can you now, before we go any further, say with all honesty, "Well, if the Lord says to stop, then I know it is for my best? I might not like it at first, but I trust he is always about protecting me, not prohibiting me, so I am convinced it will be for my best?"

I posed this scenario to many of the 721 men with whom I meet weekly, and most, even the serious disciples, had to admit, "It would feel like he is prohibiting me, not protecting me. It would color the Sabbath as a restriction, certainly not a refuge."

I understand this feeling. I felt the same way. But as you can see, that is a feeling, not a fact.

God is always for you. He is always with you. He is always out before you. He is always about protecting you from bad ideas, bad decisions, and bad actions – and protecting you from missing what is truly important. He is never about prohibiting you from having fun, or "living the life," as our empty culture promotes. Certainly not just for the sake of prohibiting you.

FACTS OVER FEELINGS

But, even though I truly believe this about God, and believe it in my heart, not just my head, as I started to dig into Sabbath-keeping, I felt like a noose was tightening around my neck. You will, too. It felt like I was losing my freedom. Like I was giving up something – dare I say it even felt like I was going to prison for the day?

Keeping the Sabbath, whatever it was going to mean, surely was not going to be any fun. However, I was undaunted in my quest to figure out God's intentions, so I abandoned my feelings and stuck to the facts.

My feelings tell me this will be restrictive. But the facts tell me God loves me and this is a gift to and for me, for a better life, a life more in harmony and balance with God – which has to be a better life, right?

By the way, feelings are horrible masters, and many of you are indeed mastered by your feelings. If I asked you to list in priority: faith – feelings – facts, how would you? Most Christians put faith first, but the truth is facts deserve top billing.

You see, your faith will waver at times, often because your feelings are taking over. At these times, we want to turn to the facts: When you are a child of God, when you have surrendered your life to Jesus as your Savior – yes, when you have been born again - the fact is you are perfectly loved, perfectly protected, and perfectly provided for in the Kingdom of God.

The facts tell me God only commands what is best for me and for you. So honoring the Sabbath has to be best – it has to be!

If we absorb this most holy truth, and only until we have, we can then take the next step in our journey to understanding the Sabbath: it is a gift from God. And we will begin to see keeping the Sabbath holy is a refuge, not a restriction. Then that noose will begin to loosen and eventually disappear.

To be replaced by a sense of joy and security.

Jesus fulfilled this when he set the legalists straight:

> "The Sabbath was made for man, not man for the Sabbath." (Mark 2:27)

A GIFT

Did you get that? "*For* man" ... as a gift *for* man ... not *against* man.

God makes a wonderful promise through Isaiah, about his gift of the Sabbath. He says,

> If you keep your feet from breaking the Sabbath and from doing as you please on my holy day, if you call the Sabbath a delight and the LORD's holy day honorable, and if you honor it by not going your own way and not doing as you please or speaking idle words,
> 14 then you will find your joy in the LORD, and I will cause you to ride on the heights of the land and to feast on the inheritance of your father Jacob.' The mouth of the LORD has spoken. (Isaiah 58:13-14)

In Chapter 9 we will expound on this passage. We will see that the call to "not do as you please" is one of our top guiding principles for our quest to keep the Sabbath set apart.

Here is how Eugene Peterson presents this passage:

> If you watch your step on the Sabbath and don't use my holy day for personal advantage, if you treat the Sabbath as a day of joy, GOD's holy day as a celebration, if you honor it by refusing 'business as usual,' making money, running here and there —
> Then you'll be free to enjoy GOD! "Oh, I'll make you ride high and soar above it all. I'll make you feast on the inheritance of your ancestor Jacob.' Yes! GOD says so. **The Message**

Do you hear God's promises? He gives us an "if-then" promise. We will discuss the "if" part much more, later, but the "then" promise is overwhelming: "Then you will ride high and soar above it all!" ... and I will cause you to ride on the heights of the land and to feast on the inheritance of your father Jacob."

Riding high and feasting is my kind of life, and I want it, don't you? More importantly, our Heavenly Father wants it for us.

This whole "keeping the Sabbath holy" thing is obviously much bigger than you or I can imagine. This is so much bigger than a list of "Can I do this?" or "You can't do that!" It is about the heart. Your heart, yes, of course, but God's heart, first and foremost.

Keeping the Sabbath is a gift from God to us, and a gateway leading into the A+ Life.

(**Note:** The A+ Life to which we constantly refer is not meant to be a prosperity gospel message. It simply means the best life God wants for you, whatever that may look like for you. Your A+ Life may be full of feasts, and mine may not. But my life will be the best possible life ... for me.)

Jesus drew battle lines across the legalistic obsession of the Pharisees with the Sabbath. And he always maintained that knowing his heart was also knowing the Father's heart, and therefore, because his Father's heart is so tender and loving, following him was never intended to be a burden, but always a gift:

"Are you tired? Worn out? Burned out on religion? Come to me. Get away with me and you'll recover your life. I'll show you how to take a real rest. Walk with me and work with me—watch how I do it. Learn the unforced rhythms of grace. I won't lay anything heavy or ill-fitting on you. Keep company with me and you'll learn to live freely and lightly." (Matthew 11:28-30 The Message)

John, Jesus' disciple and dear friend, echoed this same sentiment after only living a short time with Jesus in person, but after a lifetime of following his teachings:

"Everyone who believes that Jesus is the Christ is born of God, and everyone who loves the father loves his child as well ... 3 In fact, this is love for God: to keep his commands. **And his commands are not burdensome** ...." (1 John 5:1,3 Bold added)

When we learn to view God in this loving and gift-giving Light, it becomes a filter through which we are better able to see this Sabbath command as the gift it truly is.

Now, again, I know what you really want to say at this point: "All right, just give me a list!" ("So I can argue with it, and against it; so I can debate it; so I can ... rationalize a way to ignore it.")

But I will not give you a list, because this is not about a list of things to do or not to do, but a way for you to be. Not do or not do, be.

Jesus told the Samaritan woman at the well,

"… the true worshipers will worship the Father **in Spirit and in truth**, for they are the kind of worshipers the Father seeks." (John 4:23 Bold added)

The Spirit is how we avoid the obsession with the legalistic minutia. What does it look like to keep the Sabbath holy? It will look different for each one of us. Because we are all different. The Truth is you are to keep the Sabbath holy. The Spirit will reveal to you the intricacies for your individual life.

But only if you want him to.

The Sabbath, it seems from God's perspective, is the key to living the life … "the A+ life that is truly life." (1 Timothy 6:19 paraphrased)

After twelve Sabbaths I had only scratched the surface. But I had gone from totally blind, to beginning to glimpse this Sabbath refuge, and the gift God intends it to be.

A Sabbath Roadmap

So here is a roadmap for how we will approach our journey together, because we must do this together:

To – From: Is whatever you are considering doing on your Sabbath going to draw you to the Lord or from the Lord? This is far more important than, "Is this okay to do on Sunday?" During my Sabbath exploration, I have found some things naturally draw me towards the Lord, and others away from him.

Isaiah 58:12-13 "Do not do as you please on my holy day."

No to-do List: Do not set out to accomplish anything on this list.

Set Apart: Holy means to "set apart," so I looked for ways to set my Sundays apart. Little things, like lighting a candle on Sunday morning, not wearing a watch, sitting in a different room to spend my early morning with the Lord.

No Commerce Clause: Is God saying to us, "Please, no shopping, no going into stores, unless it's an emergency, on my day?" You may be surprised.

Not Mine: Self is my #1 combatant. I need to be reminded often I am not God, and I have found no quicker reminder than seeking to keep the Sabbath holy. Sadly, I want my way, all the time. But now, at least one day a week, I am letting God have his way with my ... oops ... his day.

Lighten Up – Tighten Up: Jesus used the Sabbath, with all its added minutia of Jewish restrictions, to deliver his favorite message: "You people have tightened up in all the wrong places: your performance - and have lightened up where it matters most: your hearts."

Guardrails: The barbarians of our noisy, frenetic and intrusive culture are at the gate, and they are never turning back. But the Sabbath can be the foundation of the garrison God will help you build to guard against these invasions.

A day set apart to the Lord, from your everyday pressing and stressing, can serve to protect you from all the electronic intrusions, busyness and clutter, and even against your Self's inner voice crying out: "Do something! Accomplish something! For crying out loud, you can't just relax all day."

Busyness and Self: We need safeguards against both.

Rhythms: Everything about our existence, our universe, even our bodies, is designed by God with a rhythm in mind. I am learning to bring the Sabbath into my life as a way of getting into his weekly rhythm, and as I have, I see how this permeates the other six days, creating a more harmonious flow, rather than a herky-jerky reacting approach to life.

Delight: In the Isaiah 58 passage God says to us, " ... if you call the Sabbath a delight ... I will reward you in unimaginable ways." What does it mean to delight in the Sabbath? Can we do this without first delighting wholeheartedly in the Lord?

Rest, Refresh, Rejuvenate, Recover: You need a break. Your mind needs a break. Your body needs a break. We all need more rest, but what a wimpy idea in this can-do culture in which we live.

Remember: God tells us to remember the Sabbath. Remember is an often-repeated word in scripture. Can you imagine why? Because we do not. We need to take time to remember who we are:

Children of God. We need to take the time to remember what he has done for us: Rescued us from a prison and a slavery of our own making. We need to take the time to remember we are human beings, not human doings.

———

One thing is for sure, the Sabbath is much bigger than just a day to rest, and it is far beyond just what we should and should not do on that day. God intends for his Sabbath to transform your life. How, I'm not sure. But I am absolutely sure that he is sure.

So rest in this knowledge that he loves you perfectly, and knows exactly what you need to flourish and thrive. You need his rest, and you need his rhythm.

You need his Sabbath.

I have spent much time in this first chapter driving home the point that God is always for you. And that God's Sabbath is a gift. I've done this because until we absorb this, and then appropriate it into our lives, the rest of this journey is a waste of time.

My desire is to shine a new light onto the Sabbath. To present to you a new way of thinking about the day, and what God is up to with his commandment. It's up to you to follow through. But I will remind you once more, the Fourth Commandment to keep the Sabbath holy is one of the most repeated commandments of all.

It must be important. To him. For you.

WAR

One last note before we begin our journey. This is war. War has been declared on your family, your togetherness, your intimacy with each other, as well as with your Heavenly Father. We did not start this war, but we have to fight it.

SABBATH LOG: SABBATH WEEK 1

Morning: Today is my first Sunday seeking to keep the Sabbath holy. I have to say I don't think I'm going to like this. It feels so restrictive. What can I do? What can I not do?

One thing I do know is that I do not want to accomplish any goals on my to-do list today.

I'm going to start with reading the two versions of the Ten Commandments: the first in Exodus 20 and the second in Deuteronomy 5.

> "Remember the Sabbath day by keeping it holy. 9 Six days you shall labor and do all your work, 10 but the seventh day is a Sabbath to the LORD your God. On it you shall not do any work, neither you, nor your son or daughter, nor your manservant or maidservant, nor your animals, nor the alien within your gates.
> 11 For in six days the LORD made the heavens and the earth, the sea, and all that is in them, but he rested on the seventh day. Therefore the LORD blessed the Sabbath day and made it holy." (Exodus 20:8-11)

> "Observe the Sabbath day by keeping it holy, as the LORD your God has commanded you. 13 Six days you shall labor and do all your work, 14 but the seventh day is a Sabbath to the LORD your God. On it you shall not do any work, neither you, nor your son or daughter, nor your manservant or maidservant, nor your ox, your donkey or any of your animals, nor the alien within your gates, so that your manservant and maidservant may rest, as you do.
> 15 Remember that you were slaves in Egypt and that the LORD your God brought you out of there with a mighty hand and an outstretched arm. Therefore the LORD

your God has commanded you to observe the Sabbath day." (Deuteronomy 5: 12-15)

Okay, this helps set my focus. It is God's day, not mine. So how to best honor him? I'll start by reading a ton of Scripture. Since I'm not preaching anywhere today, I'll just chill out all morning, take a walk, have lunch, take a nap, then perhaps take Fannie (my Golden Retriever) on another long walk at the park.

Evening: It was an okay day. I think I did pretty good, but it was boring and not particularly spiritually uplifting. I say it was boring, but in truth it wasn't that different from my previous Sundays. I guess it's just that today I felt like I *couldn't* do anything else. Like a restriction.

I took a walk with Fannie around noon, and then after a long nap took another walk with her at the park. I will say I did feel a little more relaxed, but I had this voice in my head saying, "Do something. Accomplish something!"

What a spiritual gnat I am.

2

TO – FROM

"Sabbath is that uncluttered time and space in which we can distance ourselves from our own activities enough to see what God is doing."

—Eugene Peterson

There are six days when you may work, but the seventh day is a day of sabbath rest, a day of sacred assembly. You are not to do any work; wherever you live, it is a sabbath **to the Lord**.

—Leviticus 23:3 Bold added

I HAVE ALREADY SAID GOD'S SABBATH COMMANDMENT IS one of the most repeated commandments in all of scripture – by far. It being the most repeated, why is it then the most ignored? Maybe that is a clue as to why God repeated it so often?

But let's take a moment to think about this paradox: most repeated, most ignored.

Do you think the Ten Commandments are good for us – for society? I can't imagine anyone, even atheists, arguing against the wisdom of living by the Ten Commandments. Of course no one does actually live by them, but we do at least think they are a good idea, and try to … most of the time.

Most of us at least try to avoid murder, theft, adultery, lying about others, jealously and coveting our neighbor's possessions. We try to honor our parents, even though we often do a poor job at many of these.

We at least try.

And even though we are a little fuzzy on the meaning of, "You shall have no other Gods before me," and "Do not take the Lord's name in vain," we would at least try to obey them if we could figure them out.

But the Sabbath stands alone in the Top Ten in our total ignorance of, and ignoring of this commandment.

We simply do not care about it. We think it is not applicable anymore. Not in our world. But the other nine? No one would advocate abolishing those! Yet, what kind of world would we live in if everyone actually lived by the other nine commandments? A dream world, right?

And in contrast, what kind of world would we live in if everyone ignored the other nine? A terrible mess, no doubt. Actually, we would have the kind of world and culture in which we currently live. Just to be blunt.

But if we all agree we're so much better off following, at least the best we can, the other nine commandments, why is it we feel so differently about the Sabbath commandment? Why do we totally ignore it? Why should it be any different than the others?

It is not. It is every bit as pertinent, every bit as relevant, every bit as valuable as the other nine. God's Sabbath commandment is absolutely on equal footing with the other nine, and possibly higher than the last six – if order and frequency count.

As a matter of fact, when we look at the order of the Ten Commandments, we see the first three as oriented towards God, and the last six as oriented towards man. The Fourth, as God's Sabbath, acts as a linchpin between the three God-oriented commandments and the last six man-to-man oriented commandments.

Exodus 20:

1. ³ "You shall have no other gods before me.
2. ⁴ "You shall not make for yourself an idol in the form of anything in heaven above or on the earth beneath or in the waters below. ⁵ You shall not bow down to them or worship them …
3. ⁷ "You shall not misuse the name of the LORD …
4. ⁸ **"Remember the Sabbath day by keeping it holy.**
5. ¹² "Honor your father and your mother …
6. ¹³ "You shall not murder.
7. ¹⁴ "You shall not commit adultery.
8. ¹⁵ "You shall not steal.
9. ¹⁶ "You shall not give false testimony against your neighbor.
10. ¹⁷ "You shall not covet your neighbor's house … your neighbor's wife …or anything that belongs to your neighbor."

It is as if the Lord, in his ultimate wisdom, placed this Sabbath commandment as the perfect fulcrum to support and balance the first three commandments and the last six. If our world and our lives would be so much better off if we observed and obeyed the other nine, and again, who would argue against that, you can bet the Sabbath is just as important. Ignore it at your peril. Keep it, and find the A+ life.

By the way, here is what God had to say about the reason that he gives us these commandments:

"Listen obediently, Israel. Do what you're told so that you'll have a good life, a **life of abundance and bounty**, just as God promised, in a land **abounding in milk and honey**. (Deuteronomy 6:3, bold added)

"…you'll have a good life, a life of abundance and bounty, just as God promised, in a land abounding in milk and honey." I want this, don't you? And your loving Heavenly Father wants it for you, too.

To- From

I start each Sunday morning reading the Sabbath commandment at Exodus 20 and Deuteronomy 5. It sets my focus and clarifies my purpose for this day that is God's day ... not mine. Have you read these two lately?

Two words leap out at me as I first explore God's message about the Sabbath: To and From. These help to establish a framework, a guiding principle through which you can begin to filter God's personal message to you: To and From.

The fourth commandment says this Sabbath day is ... " a Sabbath to the Lord your God." And "he rested ... *from* ... on the seventh day." Exodus 20:10, 11 (italics and *from* implied)

Anything you are considering doing on the Sabbath can be filtered through these two words: To and From:

"Will this draw me to the Lord or from the Lord?" Not, "Is what I am planning to do a violation?" But instead, "Will this take me towards the Lord, and his rest, and his purpose, or distract me away from the Lord, and his rest?"

We're not talking about going to church versus going to a strip club, but instead about weighing out options of good activities versus better/best activities. A walk in beautiful and lively downtown Greenville is nice, but a quiet walk in the woods drew me closer to the Lord.

The Sabbath is not about, "Can I do this?" but, "Is there something better I could be doing ... something perhaps that will draw me closer to my Lord, to my spouse, to my children – to myself?"

This is the first of our two major guidelines: To-From and then "Not doing as you please." (See Chapter 9)

Get it Done – Get Ahead

For example, I had been living this Sabbath-keeping for three weeks and on my third Sunday I went to the gym to work out, one of my favorite things to do on a late Sunday afternoon. Actually, it's one of my favorite things to have *gotten* done, to take off my to-do list. The *work-out* is in fact, a work-out. But the gym is quiet on a Sunday afternoon; I'm getting an extra work-out in, which puts me ahead of … somebody. Who exactly, I'm not quite sure.

You see this is an affliction of mine, and for so much of our modern culture: we need to be ahead. When driving I have this need to be ahead of the car in front of me. Even on long drives, when surely it cannot make much difference who is in front. But being ahead has got to be better than being behind, right? Of course.

This being ahead, this *getting* ahead, infiltrates much of our thinking, whether we are aware of it or not. It's part of our busyness culture. Being busy, the drive to be busy, the need to be busy, is Satan's #1 weapon against you. His rallying cry is, "If you can't make them bad, make them busy!"

More on this busyness syndrome and affliction in Chapter 6: Guardrails. But for now, let's stick to this "Being ahead" affliction.

God gave us the Sabbath as a gift: a refuge, not a restriction. A gift of freedom from work. A gift of freedom from the pressing need to be ahead at work – and work can mean anything you're doing. So my physical working out, it seems, is a part of my work life – at least for me.

How many men do I know who like to slip into the office on Sunday just to get a start on the coming week? I know some who even slip in before going to church on Sunday morning. "It's quiet, Sam, and I can get a lot done."

I think we can rest assured this Sunday morning office visit doesn't do much for preparing his heart for worship. The Sabbath becomes a perfect opportunity to get ahead in work at the office, at the gym, or whatever project in which you are involved.

So on my third Sabbath I slipped into the gym to get an extra workout in. But on my way home from my workout I heard, I sensed, the Holy Spirit whispering, "That's not what I want for you, Sam, on our Sabbath together." Now please hear this: I did not hear condemnation from God. I did not sense any anger from God, nor did I feel any guilt on my part.

I don't think I *sinned* so much, as I had simply missed it. I set out to accomplish a goal, part of my to-do list, which I am learning is in conflict with Sabbath rest.

I realized this working out was drawing me away from unity and harmony with my friend and my Savior, Jesus. Now, I know you are thinking, "So I can't go to the gym on Sundays? Now that's too legalistic."

I did not say you couldn't go to the gym. I said God whispered in my ear he didn't want me going. Possibly he won't say that to you. Perhaps he knows you don't approach working out like I do: "No pain no gain!"

So please do not start a list of what Sam says is okay and not okay, because this is not about a list of things to do or not do, but a way for us to *be*.

Again, remember Jesus told the Samaritan woman at the well,

> "... the true worshipers will worship the Father **in Spirit and in truth**, for they are the kind of worshipers the Father seeks." (John 4:23 Bold added)

Keeping the Sabbath holy will look different for each one of us. Because we are all different. The Truth is you are to keep the Sabbath holy. The Spirit will reveal to you the details for your individual life.

But only if you want him to – only if you are truly seeking to understand.

Understanding what draws you to the Lord and what pulls you away *from* him is part of our Sabbath journey. I have found it fascinating to watch God reveal his individual desire for me over these past several weeks.

To – From. Simple and direct, like God.

Is what you are considering doing on the Sabbath going to draw you closer *to* the Lord, will it enhance your harmony with your best friend and Savior, Jesus? Will it usher you into his peace and rest and rejuvenation, or will it pull you away from all of this?

As you seek to understand and appropriate this gift, this refuge, God will lovingly guide you to him, and lovingly convict you about what draws you from him. So no lists. Just Spirit and Truth. The Truth is we are to keep the Sabbath holy. The Spirit is we are to listen for God's loving guidance as to how we are to personalize this amazing gift.

Listen.

He will show you, if you want him to. He won't, if you don't.

SABBATH LOG: SABBATH WEEK 2

I started today by reading both the Exodus 20 and Deuteronomy 5 versions of the Sabbath commandment. It is amazing how this centers my thoughts and sets my perspective for the day.

But to be open and honest, I still feel like this whole "Keeping the Sabbath holy" thing is a noose around my neck, a restriction, not a refuge. I've yet to sense the refuge part. But I will say I am confident God will show me this sense of his day being a refuge, so I am undaunted! I ate leftovers at home. I did not turn the TV on until after sunset. But I did regularly look at my cell phone.

I took Fannie to the park later in the afternoon, but this time instead of walking in the woods like we normally do, we took off on the path that leads up to Main Street. If you have never been to Greenville, SC, then you just cannot appreciate how great our downtown is. Lots of restaurants and shops, and people walking around.

There might be an outdoor play going on and street musicians performing. A festive atmosphere. All fun. All positive.

But on the way back to the car I felt a conviction in my spirit, a voice from God saying, "Did this draw you towards me or away from me?"

He was right! I was not nearly as "in the moment with God" as I walked downtown, as I am when we walk in the woods. I did not feel guilty, just convicted. I thought to myself, "I can walk around Main Street any Saturday I like. But I think I'll stay away on Sundays."

The rest of the day is quiet. It's not like I do a lot on Sundays anyway. So it's not a stretch to relax.

3

THE SABBATH
COMMANDMENT ...S

"I feel as if God had, by giving the Sabbath, given fifty-two springs in each year."

—Samuel Taylor Coleridge

BE CAREFUL WHAT YOU ASK FOR

A GOOD FRIEND OF MINE, KEVIN, REMARKED THAT WHEN he first moved from California to South Carolina years ago, the state legislature was debating abolishing the Blue Laws. The Blue Laws prohibited pretty much anything fun on Sunday. No shopping except for true necessities: medicines and groceries - no alcoholic purchases whatsoever. Just about every store was closed on Sunday.

Kevin was moving from Los Angeles, California, where, as he stated, "Anything goes twenty-four hours a day seven days a week." And this was back in the early 80's, mind you.

Kevin told us that after enjoying the relaxed pace of South Carolina, and especially the shut-down mentality on Sundays, he warned everyone he encountered, "Be careful what you wish for.

You think it will be more convenient, but it will end up with your children working on Sundays, and nothing will ever be sacred again. Your families' time together will vanish."

A prophet?

EXODUS 20 – DEUTERONOMY 5

This seems like a good time to stop and look at the two Sabbath Commandments side by side. Let's compare them to see what we can glean from God's heart.

First, why two sets of Ten Commandants? The first set was given to the Israelites not long after they exited Egypt. It was at Mount Sinai and they were camped around the mountain, sort of getting their ducks in a row. Trying to figure out what this Exodus from Egypt meant, and who was this Moses and this God.

Forty years later they are on the edge of the Promise Land, about to enter. In Deuteronomy Moses takes the time before they enter the Promised Land to remind the Israelites of all God has done for them. We all need reminding, don't we? Often?

Here are the two Sabbath commandments side by side.

Exodus 20	Deuteronomy 5
⁸"**Remember** the Sabbath day by keeping it **holy:**	¹²"**Observe** the Sabbath day by keeping it **holy** as the LORD your God has commanded you.
⁹Six days you shall **labor** and do all your work: ¹⁰but the seventh day is a Sabbath **to the LORD** your God. On it you shall not do any work, neither you, nor your son or daughter, nor your manservant or maidservant, nor your	¹³Six days you shall **labor** and do all your work ¹⁴but the seventh day is a Sabbath **to the LORD** your God. On it you shall not do any work, neither you, nor your son or daughter, nor your manservant or maidservant,

animals, nor the alien within your gates.

nor … your donkey or any of your animals, nor the alien within your gates **so that** your manservant and maidservant may rest, as you do.

11 For in six days the LORD made the heavens and the earth, the sea, and all that is in them, but he rested on the seventh day:
Therefore the LORD blessed the Sabbath and made it **holy**.

15 **Remember** that you were slaves in Egypt and that the LORD your God brought you out of there with a mighty hand and an outstretched arm:
Therefore the LORD your God **has commanded** you to observe the Sabbath day.

SET APART

God identifies this day as the Sabbath, which means *rest … cease … stop*. It is interesting to me that God first refers to this seventh day as "the Sabbath" in Exodus, *after* he has delivered them from slavery.

Did you know that nowhere in the long story of the patriarchs of Genesis do we hear anything about the Sabbath? It is only until Exodus that we see God setting these Hebrews apart as his special people. Up to now we have watched him interact personally with individuals, the Patriarchs, setting these men apart as his special, called-out ones.

But now we are in the nation-building phase of God's plan, and now it becomes important for God to give his people instructions on what sets them apart from all the other nations of the world. The Sabbath is chief among these.

Up to now, we only see the Sabbath mentioned in the creation story, and there it is only referred to as the *seventh day*. God's first mention of the Sabbath is at Exodus 16, when he is feeding the Israelites for the first time, with quail in the evenings and manna in the mornings. It is here we see God setting the seventh day apart as different, special, and *holy*:

"He said to them, 'This is what the LORD commanded: 'Tomorrow is to be a day of rest, a holy Sabbath to the LORD. So bake what you want to bake and boil what you want to boil. Save whatever is left and keep it until morning.' " (Exodus 16:23)

We see God, our Heavenly Father, beginning his never-ending assurance that he is always for us, always with us, always out before us, always providing and always protecting. This becomes a constant theme throughout the scriptures. In both Exodus and the Deuteronomy God makes it clear this day is holy. Holy means to "set apart."

But in the Deuteronomy version, God adds this: "…as the LORD your God has commanded you."

I wonder why the added emphasis on "commanded"? Obviously, after forty years in the desert, they needed a reminder: "This is not just a suggestion for better living: it is my commandment to you. Because I know you, and you will not do it if I do not."

After two thousand years of living in the desert of our busyness culture, we need a reminder, too.

NO LABORING

The next part of the commandment is identical in both passages.

[9] Six days you shall **labor** and do all your work [10] but the seventh day is a Sabbath **to the LORD** you God

[13] Six days you shall **labor** and do all your work [14] but the seventh day is a Sabbath **to the LORD** your God

Here is where we see God telling us this is a day to bring you *to* the Lord. So again, a helpful guide to whatever activity you are considering for the Sabbath is to discern, "Will this draw me to the Lord, and in harmony with his rest and reverence, or away from him?"

But here God also introduces his ban against labor on the Sabbath. Now this sets off much debate among us modern Christians as to what constitutes labor. Most of this debate is not actually a debate at all - it is rationalization.

We don't want any intrusion on our freedom to do whatever we want to do whenever we want to do it, so we have become experts at rationalizing whatever supports what we want to do. And it is no different with this labor on the Sabbath debate. But I do acknowledge this labor term can be vague and ambiguous. So let's make it as simple as possible.

Labor certainly means not going into the office, or performing any functions related to your profession. Can we at least agree on this? I think labor is anything you have to work at. Beyond this, I like Eugene Peterson's idea: Labor ... work ... is anything you don't really want to do. Eugene also says labor is accomplishing things.

Yet even this is sticky, because my friends who want to work in the yard, cut their grass and all that, say this is not work for them. They say it is restful for them, and invigorating to work in the yard. Some say it even brings them closer to God.

They may be right about that. But I ask them, is working in the yard as restful as sitting on the porch talking with your family? Is running your lawnmower as peaceful, as relaxing as taking a nap, reading a book, or perhaps even reading scripture? Is your leaf blower restful and peaceful; for your neighbor?

Their response? An irritated glare.

Now let me say quickly I am not saying that working in your yard is against the "rules." Remember, please, I am not putting forth any rules at all. But we must admit we rationalize all kinds of activity on our Sabbaths, simply because we want to do whatever we want to do. Perhaps it is more accurate to say we want to *have done* it - to have ... gotten ahead?

To me, labor is anything at which I have to *labor*. Simple enough? Working out is labor for me. Sure, it's invigorating and refreshing, but is a workout. It is labor. So do not labor on your Sabbath. If you do you're simply missing the point. It is not so much that you are breaking a rule, as it is you're just missing the harmony and balance, and the sanctity of the Sabbath.

The question to ask yourself is not, "Is this okay to do on the Sabbath?" The better question is, "Is this the best thing I could be doing?"

A "No Commerce" Clause?

God loves you dearly, but he still knows you need more help on the no-labor idea, so he expands. The Exodus and Deuteronomy passages are virtually identical, but in the Deuteronomy passage God drills down a little deeper with a "so that" explanation:

> " ...**so that** your manservant and maidservant may rest, as you do."

Exodus 20	Deuteronomy 5
On it you shall not do any work,	On it you shall not do any work,
neither you, nor your son or daughter nor your manservant or maidservant, nor your animals, nor the alien within your gates.	neither you, nor your son or daughter, nor your manservant or maidservant, nor ... your donkey or any of your animals, nor the alien within your gates **so that** your manservant and maidservant may rest ... (*from*), as you do. (Added)

This "so that" sounds an awful lot like a "No Commerce" clause, wouldn't you agree? Okay, now we are really starting to meddle, and I can already hear the howls coming from you. But read it for yourself:

> "Don't work, nor make anyone else over whom you have any authority work, nor do anything that may

cause them to work, "so that" they can rest as well, and won't have to work, either." (Paraphrase)

But this no-commerce clause is nothing new. Nehemiah, writing twenty-five hundred years ago (circa 450 BC) sounds as though he is observing any city in the U.S., on any given Sunday:

"In those days I saw men in Judah treading winepresses on the Sabbath and bringing in grain and loading it on donkeys, together with wine, grapes, figs and all other kinds of loads. And they were bringing all this into Jerusalem on the Sabbath. Therefore I warned them against selling food on that day.
16 Men from Tyre who lived in Jerusalem were bringing in fish and all kinds of merchandise and selling them in Jerusalem on the Sabbath to the people of Judah. 17 I rebuked the nobles of Judah and said to them, "What is this wicked thing you are doing--desecrating the Sabbath day?
18 Didn't your forefathers do the same things, so that our God brought all this calamity upon us and upon this city? Now you are stirring up more wrath against Israel by desecrating the Sabbath." (Nehemiah 13:15-18)

We today are no different than these Sabbath workers twenty-five hundred years ago. Nor is the damage it is doing. So God insists, "You are not to do commerce on the Sabbath, so your manservants and maidservants, nor anyone, else has to, either."

I don't have any manservants and maidservants anymore. Do you? I got rid of mine when the economy went south. All kidding aside, the modern-day application is that we are not to do anything on the Sabbath that may cause someone else to have to work. I know this is highly controversial, not to mention invasive, to our "do what we want when we want" attitude. And I know if I go out to eat on a

Sabbath I'm not technically causing the wait staff and cooks to have to work; they will be there anyway.

But I don't want to live in the "everyone else is doing it" world any longer, do you? That is the classic C- life for sure. I have found it is safe, and richly rewarding, as with anything God asks me to do, to obey him. So I try to.

Not going into stores of any kind does indeed set the day apart, perhaps like nothing else I could do – or not do – on the Sabbath. It is inconvenient at times, but I am more and more getting into the simple habit of shopping for my Sunday meals on Saturday. And reminding myself to do this is yet another reminder that God is in charge of my life, not me.

RELATIONSHIP OVER RULES

Let's pause just for a moment and look at a truth I hear Jesus saying throughout his ministry: "Relationship overrides rules, always." We'll discuss this much more in Chapter 5: Lighten Up-Tighten Up. But for now, if you have an ox in the ditch, and you need to go into a store, go. If eating out engenders relationship, and it is an exception, not an every-Sabbath norm, then pursue the relationship.

Don't be legalistically bull-headed about it. But also remember that exceptions become the norm very quickly, and just as quickly you will find yourself right back where you were before. So ponder this "No Commerce" clause carefully. I have found during my Sabbath journey there are many times it would be very convenient to go into a store or restaurant, but not necessary.

There is a big difference between convenient and necessary.

HERE'S WHY

God proceeds to give us the reason behind the Sabbath commandment to rest – and there are two of them. In Exodus he is saying, "I did, so you do, too." In Deuteronomy he is saying, "The Sabbath is a reminder you were a slave, don't ever be one again."

Exodus 20	Deuteronomy 5
[11] For in six days the LORD made the heavens and the earth, the sea, and all that is in them, but he rested on the seventh day:	[15] **Remember** that you were slaves in Egypt and that the LORD your God brought you out of there with a mighty hand and an outstretched arm:

In the Exodus passage, God says I rested on the Sabbath, so you do, too. If God rested, and asks me to do the same, that's good enough for me. We can debate what exactly constitutes work in the "No-labor / No-commerce" clause portion of this Sabbath commandment, but can we at least agree there is no debating God's direct statement here?

"I rested. You rest, too."

Now in the Deuteronomy passage, Eugene Peterson observes this about the reason God gives us:

> "The reason given here for Sabbath-keeping is different than that given in Exodus. In Exodus we are told to keep the Sabbath because God kept it. Since he rested on the seventh day, we should also rest on that day, getting back in step with the creation rhythms of work and rest. "In Deuteronomy, however, we're told keeping Sabbath is a matter of simple justice; it prevents the stronger from exploiting the weaker, whether parents over children or employers over employees. Each of us is given a day to recover the simple dignity of being ourselves in the community without regard to function or status." (The Message Study Bible)

The Deuteronomy passage is also a reminder. After forty years the Israelites needed to be reminded they were once slaves. Don't you? Because you were.

Do Not Drift

*It is for freedom that Christ has set us free. Stand firm, then,
and do not let yourselves be burdened again by a yoke of slavery.*

—Galatians 5:1

I was certainly a slave to many gods before Jesus stepped in and
saved me. And of course I remained a semi-slave for years, even as
the little gods faded, and my Savior increased. I can still revert to
slavery, quickly, if I don't remind myself I've been rescued and freed
from all and any kind of slavery by Jesus, my Savior.

I can so easily again become a slave to our culture. Allowing
myself to become a slave again always ends up, without exception,
a disappointing mess. I can become a slave again to Self, which is
my #1 combatant – and yours too. Much more on Self in Chapter 6
on Guardrails.

I can become a slave again to what others think. Ugh. I can become a slave again to old habits. I can become a slave again to old
idols, which are always lurking around, ready to assume their
throne of importance in my life.

And I can become a slave again to Satan, who is the mastermind
behind all the previous slave masters I just mentioned. But what
type of slavery is God addressing in his Sabbath commandment?

The "If I don't, it won't" Syndrome

One of your deadliest enemies, and potential slave masters, is the "If
I don't, it won't" syndrome – the "If it's to be, it's up to me!" This is
dominant among men but inflicts you ladies as well. This syndrome,
sickness is a better word, maybe even addiction, is that voice in your
head warning you, "You better take care of this yourself. You cannot
trust God, at least not in this situation. If you don't take action to
control this it might not turn out like you want it to."

This, "If I don't make it happen, if I don't force it, control it, strangle it, manipulate it, or just take it for myself, then it won't happen the way it must for me to be happy," is just a slight variation on Satan's words to Adam and Eve:

"Really, did God say not to eat from that tree? Oh come on, he's just trying to prohibit you from the good life. What, you think he's about protecting you from something? Don't be ridiculous. I know God better than you. He really cannot be trusted. Listen to me: if you want to get it right, if you want to make things happen like they should, you need to take control of this situation."

And off they went on the path to destruction. All from the "If I don't, it won't" syndrome.

So our loving and caring Heavenly Father, who knows and wants what is best for us, warns us and reminds us just how easily we can slip back to becoming slaves again. His Sabbath day off from labor is a wonderful way to keep our freedom.

If you learn to relax, and rest, and rejuvenate on the Sabbath, and if you master the need to work ... oh, come on, just a little ... to get ahead, you will see just how valuable this commandment truly is for your harmony and rhythm.

THEREFORE

God ends the Sabbath commandment in both the Exodus and Deuteronomy passages with a "therefore": i.e. "This is what I have previously said is *there for*."

Exodus 20	Deuteronomy 5
Therefore the LORD blessed the Sabbath and made it **holy**	**Therefore** the LORD your God **has commanded** you to observe the Sabbath day.

Remember Jesus told the Samaritan woman at the well "... the true worshipers will worship the Father **in Spirit and in truth**, for they are the kind of worshipers the Father seeks." (John 4:23 Bold added)

This Exodus version is from the Spirit: "I made this day holy, so you set it apart from all your other days of the week. I did, so you do, too."

The Deuteronomy version is the Truth: "This is not just a good suggestion for A+ living; it is *a commandment.*"

SABBATH LOG: SABBATH WEEK 3

I started today by reading both the Exodus 20 and Deuteronomy 5 version of the Sabbath commandment. It is amazing how this centers my thoughts and sets my perspective for the day.

What can I do today that "sets apart" this day? I ponder this for a while and can only think of small things, such as not wearing my watch today. Now I know this seems silly, but I am a tad OCD and I look at my watch often. So I hope each time I check the time and see my watch is not there it will remind me today is different.

I need a lot of reminding, that is for sure.

I think I'll also do my Bible reading and praying in a different room than I do Monday – Saturday. I'll go in the Living Room. Just another small way to set the morning apart.

After guest-preaching today I stopped by the grocery store, and immediately felt a halt in my spirit. I go to this same grocery store about once a week, typically on Mondays or Tuesdays. I have never seen it this crowded! It was a mass of people, most of whom were dressed in their Sunday church clothes.

I asked the store manager about the crowd and he nonchalantly said, "Oh, Sundays are our busiest time – especially in this store." (This store being in the higher socio-economic neighborhood, by the way)

I felt as though I was surrounded by Churchians, not Christians. Surrounded by people who follow church, not Christ. The Sabbath was being wholly decimated by this surge to shop, and I was right there with them. I wish I could describe the check in my spirit, but I got out of there as soon as I could and I do not plan to do that again.

I could only imagine that they were shopping on Sunday so as to not interfere with their Saturday – their day.

From that point forward I almost never go into a grocery store on Sundays, and when I do, for relationship, I actually feel as though I am going into a strip club. Yes, it has made that kind of conviction in my heart.

4

SUSPICIOUS MINDS

Why can't you see
What you're doing to me
When you don't believe a word I say?

We can't go on together
With suspicious minds
And we can't build our dreams
On suspicious minds.

—Elvis

Jesus: "A certain man was preparing a great banquet and in-
vited many guests. But they all alike began to make excuses."

—Luke 14:1

AS I HAVE SAID, WHEN I FIRST STARTED MENTIONING to my friends that I was convicted about this Sabbath thing, I got some unexpected reactions. Mostly hostile. They were suspicious of God's motives behind the Sabbath.

It was obvious they felt the noose tightening, just as I had. But why the pushback? Clearly I was intruding on their territory. They felt threatened by this Sabbath talk, but threatened by what?

God's commandment to "Keep the Sabbath holy," even in the Bible-belt of the South, goes largely unnoticed, and is considered by most to be unnecessary and unwelcome -and certainly irrelevant. As I was teaching on this over the first several weeks in our 721 meetings, the reactions I had received, and the excuses, (some being my own) have at times bordered on ludicrous.

Many were suspicious of me. Many of you are, too. I encouraged them, as I encourage you, to talk to God about it. It's his commandment, not mine.

But of course I can absolutely relate, because as I mentioned early on, when I began my own personal journey into the Sabbath I felt like it was all doom and gloom, a restriction, not a refuge. I felt God was meddling and prohibiting me from ... my right to myself!

And I was suspicious of his motives.

But God promises us at Isaiah 58: "... if you call the Sabbath a delight ... you will **feast** on the inheritance of your father Jacob ..."2

God promises a Sabbath feast!

EXCUSES

Jesus tells the story of another great feast, but those invited weren't interested, or like so many I've encountered, "they all alike began to make excuses." (Luke 14:16-17)

So I present here is a modern day "**Parable of Suspicions and Excuses**:"

I want you to imagine someone in a position of influence in your life: it's your boss if you have one – or it's your most lucrative client, or the judge before whom you try cases, your business partner, or whoever fits your particular scenario. Use your imagination.

He calls you into his office and says this:

"You are so valuable to me, and so important. I want you to have the best life possible. I want you to be at your best at all times

– for yourself, as well as for your family and your God. I want this for you because you cannot be at your best for me if you are not at your best in these other areas.

"So, in order for you to both experience the best life possible, and to produce the best life possible, I am hereby commanding you to … take one full day off a week. On that day I want you to relax, totally relax. I do not want to see you out running errands to catch up. I do not want to hear about you working on that day in order to get ahead. Do not even think about coming into the office. I better not see you here!"

He continues, "I do not expect to see you in the grocery store, or even dining out, getting gas in your car, or anything having to do with commerce. That will only distract you from my goal: a totally relaxed body and a clear mind for you.

"You see my dear friend, I have learned that for me to get the best out of you, you must be experiencing the best for yourself. And when that happens, we both win."

Now a smile spreads across his face and he says, "I am commanding you to take this day, because you are important *to* me, and I know how important this is *for* you. For you to produce at the highest level, and therefore to experience the highest level of the A+ Life that is truly Life, I want you rested, and relaxed, and rejuvenated.

"Anyone who is in harmony and in balance in their body-mind-spirit will be at their best, and will live at their best. This day off I'm commanding you to take will actually give you incredible power: increased energy, increased clarity, and don't miss this: increased creativity.

"If you obey my command and take this day off, I will not only pay you, and provide for you, but I will also bless you in ways you cannot even begin to imagine. You will receive bonuses in every aspect of life. Trust me; I will bless you, your marriage, and your entire family."

With a serious look he then leans across the table and says, "But you must abide by my command to rest, relax, rejuvenate, and reflect. On this day I hope you will think about what's truly important to you, what the A+ Life really looks like. Reflect on how much you are already blessed. Reflect on what I've already done for you throughout your life.

"Remember, no work, no labor, no to-do lists to accomplish – simply put, no distractions and no anxiety. Just relax."

You've sat quietly, listening to a man you normally trust without hesitation, but now you're suspicious of his motives.

You're absolutely shocked at what an obnoxious and inconsiderate boss you have! What a demanding, intruding man he is. How dare he meddle in your personal affairs like this? You have the right to do with your time what you want, when you want, however you want.

You know what is best for you, and taking a day off like this is just ridiculous.

You will not stand for it! You quit on the spot!

Can you see yourself in this, and how we react to God's Sabbath commandment in this modern-day parable? I hope so, because as absurd as our reaction sounds, this is the reaction I have been getting.

And here are a host of other objections I've heard (some Sam's) to this blatant meddling command from this obviously control-crazed God:

What, I can't play golf that day?

You are a fanatic!

Do I have to tell my wife about this? She might not like it and blame me. She might think *I'm* a fanatic.

We have small children so this is impossible. What about travel ball?? Dance practice??

You are out of touch with reality. It's like you're living in archaic, Old Testament times.

This is just totally unrealistic.

You expect me to just waste a day, accomplishing nothing?

This won't be any *fun*.

But Sunday is the best day to: do some shopping or to catch up on all the things on my list, or even to get ahead for next week.

You expect me to do ... nothing? Where's the catch?

I'm not ready for this kind of commitment.

Am I going to end up having to stand on the street corner and preach to everyone about this?

No day should be any different than the others. I should be living in harmony and balance each day, so I'm going to ignore you. (Of course I'm not actually living this way, but that's irrelevant.)

But I get fulfillment out of working, that's how I find my identity and self-worth.

I don't know how to relax and take a day off.

Nap? I've never been able to take naps. (Perhaps indicative of a deeper issue?)

Whoa, whoa, whoa, we live in an age of grace, so I'm forgiven if I ignore the Sabbath.

And my personal favorite: "I'll need a complete list of what I can do, and what I cannot do, before I decide to accept your offer."

And Jesus said: "They all alike began to make excuses. I tell you, not one of those who were invited will get a taste of my banquet." (Luke 14:24)

The Sabbath is a banquet. Taste it.

More Objections

Here are the three most repeated objections I've heard, even from Godly people:

"I don't know why we have to study this; it's Old Testament stuff, and Jesus came to replace all that."

From a pastor friend, who no doubt loves the Lord: "Oh, I don't know about that – we live in an age of grace."

(An age of grace. So? What does grace have to do with a gift? That is, of course, unless one is thinking of the Sabbath as a restriction, not a refuge.)

More than one Godly man, and I mean truly Godly men, reacted with: "Well Jesus is our new Sabbath. Now every day should be a Sabbath day for a follower of Christ."

These men meant it, and they no doubt thought it was true - and it is. Every day should be like a Sabbath day for the disciple of Jesus. But it is not, and it likely will not ever be. Not as long as we are living in this culture of work and busyness.

It's a nice thought; it is just not realistic.

After weeks of seeking to understand what "Keeping the Sabbath holy" means, I was still wandering around clumsily. My Sabbath-keeping was very much a work in progress. But there was progress, and the fog was lifting. I was starting to see this gift as the "immeasurably, abundantly more than anything we can ask for or even imagine to ask for" kind of gift it is. (Ephesians 3:20 paraphrased)

Yet so many are pushing back. A favorite refrain is, "But Jesus did away with the Old Testament law. This is the New Testament; we live in an age of grace."

Let's pause and examine the relevancy of the Older Testament versus the New Testament.

5

LIGHTEN UP – TIGHTEN UP

THE "NEW TESTAMENT JESUS" COMES ALONG AND STARTS his ministry by clarifying his teaching mission:

"Do not think that I have come to abolish the Law or the Prophets; I have not come to abolish them but to fulfill them." (Matthew 5:17)

He then proceeds to *fulfill* the Sabbath commandment by knocking the props out from under the Pharisees' legalistic approach to the Sabbath. But if you think Jesus is abolishing the Sabbath, please think again.

Jesus is saying, "Lighten up but tighten up: Lighten up you stiff-necked legalists, you've lost the heart of my Father; but tighten up, you who think you can ignore my commandments. All my laws are about the heart, first, but they are still *commandments*."

In Jesus' Sermon on the Mount, he admonishes us to tighten up where it counts the most: our heart. If you will read the Sermon on the Mount (Matthew 5-7), you will see Jesus repeatedly exposes the hypocritical way the legalists approach the Older Testament commandments. They are very tight on their technical obedience, but way too loose in their hearts.

As a contrast from the Older Testament laws to Jesus' heart view, consider these comparisons from Jesus' Sermon on the Mount (Matthew 5-6):

Is it easier to not kill or to not get angry? (Tighten up on your anger)

Easier to not commit adultery or to not lust? (Tighten up on your lust)

Easier to swear an oath or "simply let your 'yes' be 'yes' and your 'no' be 'no'?" (Tighten up on your swearing promises and your excessive self-vindication)

Is it easier to revenge an eye for an eye or to turn the other cheek … to love your neighbor or to love your enemy … to forgive once or to forgive over and over? (Tighten up on your heart)

Can you see these are all about Tighten Up?

Jesus' Sermon on the Mount is all about "Lighten up but tighten up."

When we see how Jesus plows right over our keenly crafted rationalizations and our carefully arranged loopholes, we might just long for the 'rigid' Older Testament approach. At least then we could ignore the spirit of the law, as long as we keep the legal part.

But Jesus tells us,

> "… the true worshipers will worship the Father **in Spirit and in truth**, for they are the kind of worshipers the Father seeks." (John 4:23 Bold added)

So no loopholes and no rationalizations.

Again, the Truth is: "keeping the Sabbath holy" is a commandment. The Spirit is: God's Holy Spirit will show you the heart of this commandment, and how it applies individually to you.

Mark tells us a story about the Pharisees and the teachers of the law – a "tight" group if ever there was one – complaining to Jesus that his disciples did not observe the rituals of washing their hands before eating:

> "So the Pharisees and teachers of the law asked Jesus, 'Why don't your disciples live according to the tradition

of the elders instead of eating their food with 'unclean' hands?'"

Jesus was not exactly pleased with their tightness:

"He replied,
'Isaiah was right when he prophesied about you hypocrites; as it is written: " 'These people honor me with their lips, but their hearts are far from me. 7 They worship me in vain; their teachings are but rules taught by men.' 8 You have let go of the commands of God and are holding on to the traditions of men.'" (Mark 7:5-8)

Jesus is saying, "You are too tight in the wrong areas and way too loose where it counts: your heart."

But Jesus is not done with them. To drive his point home about Tighten Up – Lighten Up, he makes sure he has the crowd's attention before continuing. Here we see the clear difference between Lighten up and Tighten up:

Lighten Up: Mark 7:14 " … Listen to me, everyone, and understand this. 15 Nothing outside a person can defile them by going into them. - Rather, it is what comes out of a person that defiles them." 17 After he had left the crowd and entered the house, his disciples asked him about this parable. 18 "Are you so dull?" he asked. "Don't you see that nothing that enters a person from the outside can defile them? 19 For it doesn't go into their heart but into their stomach, and then out of the body." (In saying this, Jesus declared all foods clean.)

Tighten Up: Mark 7:20 He went on: "What comes out of a person is what defiles them. 21 For it is from within, out of a person's heart, that evil thoughts come—sexual immorality, theft, murder, 22 adultery, greed, malice, deceit, lewdness, envy, slander, arrogance and folly. 23 All these evils come from inside and defile a person."

Do you see the delineation Jesus is making? What you eat, or watch, or do (within the moral guidelines your Father has set for your good) is not what makes you clean before God. If that were the case King David would be burning in Hell right now.

No! As in all things, it is a matter of the heart: "What comes out of a person is what defiles them."

I sort of wish he had not made such a clear distinction. You see, I can *perform* outwardly much better than I can be inwardly. What you can see me doing is much easier for me to manage. But what is in my heart, oh, the darkness lurking within there.

OUTWARD PERFORMANCE – INWARD HEART

Let's stop for a moment and examine this phenomenon of outward performance versus inward heart.

Why am I so much better at the things I know others will see? Because "what others think" is a huge affliction with me – and I bet you, as well. Sadly, even after walking with the Lord for eighteen years now, if I am not constantly checking my heart, my chief concern is what others think.

I desire to have only an audience of one: God. But I so easily slip back into performing for what others think about me.

But God looks in our heart. Not because that is the easiest place to catch us, but because he knows, as we all do, this is the real issue. If I say something crass, or mean-spirited or judgmental, I quickly exclaim, "I don't know where that came from!"

The obvious answer is, "It came from my heart."

Ugh.

Another Lighten up – Tighten Up example:

Tighten Up: Matthew 16:24 Then Jesus said to his disciples, "Whoever wants to be my disciple must deny themselves and take up their cross and follow me."

But Lighten Up: Matthew 11:28 "Come to me, all you who are weary and burdened, and I will give you rest. 29 Take my yoke upon you and learn from me, for I am gentle and humble in heart, and you will find rest for your souls. 30 For my yoke is easy and my burden is light." (Bold added)

Jesus is saying, "Tighten up my friends, because following me is going to require you to confront and deny your #1 combatant, Self. And you will have to do it daily, die to it daily, if you want to follow me into the A+ life that is truly life."

But he also says, "Lighten up, because this is going to be the best life you could ever imagine. So don't get down about what may seem like an uphill battle. As you confront and deny your Self, you will begin to see clearly how much I am for you.

"Tighten up, but lighten up, because 'My yoke is easy and my burden is light.'"

So when the Pharisees went nuts over Jesus' disciples picking a few pieces of grain on a Sabbath, he responded with an incredulous,

> "There is far more at stake here than religion. If you had any idea what this Scripture meant—'I prefer a flexible heart to an inflexible ritual'—you wouldn't be nitpicking like this. The Son of Man is no lackey to the Sabbath; he's in charge." (Matthew 12:6-8 The Message)

Can't you just hear Jesus saying, "Lighten up, it's about your heart, not a ritual, and surely not a restriction? But tighten up, because I am still in charge of the Sabbath. And I am *commanding* you to rest, relax, remember, refresh, rejuvenate, rejoice on this Holy day."

Don't ignore the Sabbath, explore it. See what God has in store for you. Just try it. Start with waking up and saying, "Today is the Sabbath. It's God's day." Just start with that. And maybe, just maybe, put your to-do list aside, just for a day. Try it, it's not that scary.

Accomplish … nothing. Play, and pray more.

DET BOWERS - TIM KELLER - EUGENE PETERSON

In Chapter 3 we commented on the "No Commerce" clause of the Sabbath Commandment. This seems like a good place to delve a little deeper into that idea, as we examine the Tighten Up – Lighten Up message of Jesus.

There are widely varied interpretations among bona fide Jesus followers about this No Commerce clause. Some will appear to be all about tightening up, i.e. don't do anything. Others, like Eugene Peterson, may appear to be all about Lightening up, relaxing, and enjoying the day.

DET BOWERS

My pastor friend Det Bowers takes what most would say is a very conservative view. Tim Keller, the preacher and founder of Re-deemer Presbyterian Church in Manhattan, seems to be a bit more to the center. Eugene Peterson, if we are considering a spectrum, even more so to the looser end than Tim Keller.

I have read and listened to all three of these men extensively, and find them to be sold-out, sincerely committed followers of Jesus, and exceptionally Godly men, seeking to know and please God. But they differ in their application of this No Commerce clause in the Sabbath commandment.

My friend Det Bowers has a strict interpretation: Basically, do not do anything other than rest and worship.

This came into play several years ago when one of Det's sons was younger and playing baseball. He was one of the best players on the team. The team was in the championship game on a Saturday afternoon, but the game was rain-delayed until the following day – a Sunday.

In Det's mind there was no ambiguity: We don't play organized sports on the Sabbath.

You can imagine the uproar this caused. "How can you do this to us?" "But it's not fair to the other boys!" "We can't win without your son!"

Det was undaunted.

Like it or not, and I'm sure most of you do not, imagine the lesson his son learned from his father's conviction. He might or might not have remembered the game if he had played, but you can bet he remembers his father's stand.

So do I. And all these years later, God used Det's reverence for the Sabbath – even if at the time I did not like it - to capture my attention, and now hopefully yours.

TIM KELLER

Tim Keller seems to take a more moderate approach to activities on the Sabbath.

> Take some sheer inactivity time. Almost everyone needs some time every week that is so un-planned and un-structured that you do whatever you spontaneously feel like doing. If your Sabbath time is simply a very busy time filled with scheduled activities of recreation and ministry, it will not suffice. There must be some cessation from exertion.
>
> Take some avocational time. An avocation is something that is sheer pleasure to you, but that takes some exertion and time and usually is something that others do 'for a living.'
>
> You need recreational rest. The Puritans and others were rightly skeptical of recreations that forced you or others to spend a great deal of money and time and exertion. Be careful that recreation really refreshes.
>
> You need aesthetic rest. You need to expose yourselves to works of God's creation that refresh and energize you, that you find beautiful. This may mean out-of-doors things. This may also mean art, music, drama, visual art. (Sabbath Rest and Work MCM February, 2003)

EUGENE PETERSON

Eugene Peterson, who first piqued my interest in the Sabbath with his obvious enthusiasm and love for the day, told us in our New York seminar, "Sabbath is for playing and praying." I've included some of the notes I took while listening to Eugene expound on the Sabbath below.

PRACTICES THAT GROUND US

If we take care of the moments, the years will take care of themselves. And the Sabbath is a primary reminder, and tool, to learn to take care of the moments

Coach people to Sabbath not teach them to Sabbath. And never out of guilt; help them to learn how to Sabbath in *their* context. They can find a way!

The practice of Sabbath permeates our lives, instead of just one day

What does it mean to Sabbath? "Shut up and show up"

Start not with the Sabbath but with God. When we don't keep the Sabbath we're trying to be like gods

The Sabbath is uncluttered time and space to distance ourselves from our own frenzy

As to what he often did on Sundays: After worship I might drink a beer, then take a liturgical nap. Then take walks. Nothing organized!

If one is not an outdoors nature guy, how to Sabbath in other ways: some of his friends go to movies, museums, sporting events, concerts (Obviously no, "No Commerce clause," here)

My kids didn't have to clean their rooms.

I didn't do anything I didn't have to. The Sabbath is about freedom, not guilt.

Anything that is work for you, don't do it. Sabbath-keeping is to enjoy, and therefore to learn to enjoy life

At church on Sundays: We held no meetings! No programs:

Eugene writes in *Christ Plays In Ten Thousand Places*:

"Pastors and congregational leaders commonly cram the Lord's Day with work: committees, meetings, projects, mission and social activities. Much doing and much talking displace Sabbath quietness, and stillness.

"Typically congregational leaders, knowing that they have these people all to themselves for a few hours on just one day a week, conspire to get them involved in anything and everything they think will be good for their souls and good for the church.

"Well-intentioned but dead wrong. All the leaders do is get them so busy for the Lord that they have no time for the Lord, pour in so much information about God that they never have a chance to listen to God." (*Christ Plays In Ten Thousand Places* page 118)

PLAYING & PRAYING

Playing is important because it's not necessary. You don't *have* to play – if you have to play, it's not play

Praying: Sabbath is more than just a day off – prayer is part of the Sabbath

Learn to pray into a rhythm of what God is doing, not what you are doing

Sabbath-keeping is anything you don't have to do … anything you can lose yourself in

My (Eugene's) goal is not to master 'prayer techniques', but to live a life suffused by prayer so my life is prayer.

SIMPLICITY

Eugene spoke that day on simplicity, which is of course an integral part of the Sabbath life:

Simplicity starts in the heart and works its way out

We are looking for a life that is not competitive, but contemplative

Eugene talked about his annual trip to a monastery. The Benedictine Monks would always say at the beginning of his time there: "If you realize there's something you need and don't have it, ask one of the Brothers and he'll show you have to do without it."

And, " Stay in your cell – your cell will teach you everything. Find ways to be in the moment, to pay attention to the moment. Pay attention to what's there, not what's not there.

Eugene concluded his comments that afternoon with: Shalom life: content with who you are, where you are. We need constant purging: who am I? What is God's plan for me?   Shalom: whole, connected, integrated.

ROB BELL

Rob Bell, somewhat in the Eugene Peterson camp, puts it this way: "Along with rest and reverence, do whatever feeds your soul." (Everything is Spiritual)

Now I know you do not like some of what you are reading right now, and trust me, I understand. Maybe I am wrong about God's No Commerce clause. I can only say this is what God has told me. As we have already said, the true worshipers worship in Spirit and Truth. The Truth is God said, "Do not cause anyone to work on his Sabbath." The Spirit will show you how this applies to you, individually.

That is, if you want him to. So I'm not sneaking in any rules about the Sabbath. I'm simply pointing out what God clearly states, and how he spoke to me.

On a humorous note, my friend Cubby told me he was having his house painted, and the painter wanted to work on Sunday. Cub,

being a Sabbath observer, told the painter he didn't want him working at his house on a Sunday.

But Cubby was worried he was depriving the man of income,
and said so. The painter smiled and said, "Oh don't worry, I can
paint down the street at the Baptist preacher's house."

RELATIONSHIP TRUMPS RULES

I must be transparent here. I adhere to the "Relationship trumps
Rules" message at various times on the Sabbath. If my daughter is
coming through town, I will get her favorite chips and salsa from
the neighborhood Mexican restaurant. Or if I am visiting her, we will
go out for a meal.

I have eaten Sunday brunch with friends when it was clear to
me it would enhance our relationship, and give me the chance to be
an influence for Jesus in their lives. But hear this: I do not do this
lightly, nor do I do it often. I am fully aware of the tendency and
how quickly exceptions become the norm.

I see this "Relationship trumps Rules" as part of the Lighten Up
–Tighten Up message from Jesus. If I were to carry legalism to the
extreme, imagine I get a call from one of the men in our weekly
groups asking me to drive the forty-five miles to his home to help
with a pressing problem with, say, his marriage, or a child, or any
host of personal crises.

How do you think Jesus would feel if I responded, "Well, I'd
like to help, but it's the Sabbath, and I'm too low on gas to make it
over there without stopping for gas, and I strictly adhere to No Commerce on the Sabbath approach. So no can do."

Do you think this would please Jesus?

Remember, Jesus said, quoting God, "I desire a flexible heart to
an inflexible routine." (Matthew 12:7 The Message)

I have even gone to the gym late on Sunday afternoon on two
occasions, both times after it had rained all weekend, and I was going stir-crazy after being inside all day. However, again, please hear

this: I do not do any of these things lightly and without at least some thought and discussion with the Lord.

Personally, I must profess that not doing commerce on the Sabbath has helped to set this day apart – to make it holy, for me, and for my Father. I am grateful God opened my eyes.

SABBATH LOG: SABBATH WEEK 4

My friend Irv is facing a firestorm. His son Bubba is a good athlete, especially in basketball. The basketball coach at his high school is also the travel squad coach. Of course the travel squad plays on weekends and that includes Sundays. Irv is resolute in not participating in organized sports on the Sabbath, so he will not allow Bubba to play in the Sunday games.

The coach will not stand for it, and has stated bluntly to Irv, "If Bubba doesn't play on Sundays he will not start on the high school varsity team" – which he otherwise would. So Irv's conviction to honor the Sabbath, to set it apart from all the other days, is costing Bubba a starting position.

Bubba understands and respects his father's decision, but I can tell you that it is killing Irv to be the cause of his son's suffering. I think I should dedicate this book to Irv, because I am not facing anything like such pain and suffering.

6

GUARDRAILS

"The Sabbath both dethrones and dignifies us."

—Darrin Patrick

THERE WILL ALWAYS BE QUESTIONS ABOUT THE SABBATH. Hopefully you will soon move past suspicions, and move towards "acceptance, without exception." Jesus, in his most wonderful way, simplifies all our issues about any of our questions, with his invitation, "Come to me, and you will see."

Listen to Oswald Chambers' thoughts on this:

> "The questions that truly matter in life are remarkably few, and they are all answered by these words — "Come to Me." Our Lord's words are not, "Do this, or don't do that," but — "Come to me." If I will simply come to Jesus, my real life will be brought into harmony with my real desires. I will actually cease from sin, and will find **the song of the Lord** beginning in my life." (My Utmost For His Highest June 11 – bold added)

> " ... will find the song of the Lord beginning in my life:"

This is what God is promising through his Sabbath. But we so often miss this precious song, because we have wandered off track. We find ourselves in the desert; we're lost. How did this happen? We drifted.

As the Eagles say, "We are like sheep without a shepherd, we don't know how to be alone. So we wander around this dessert, following the wrong gods home." (Learn to be Still)

DRIFTING

> *We must pay the most careful attention, therefore, to what we have heard, so that we do not drift away.*
>
> —Hebrews 2:1

Drifting is a common affliction among all of us. Disciples of Jesus are no exception. No one wakes up one day and says, "Today I am going to start a series of decisions that will ultimately lead to a disaster in my life." No one abruptly decides to start ignoring God in their lives. Rarely does anyone decide to stop reading their Bibles, or spend time in prayer, or step away from Jesus' guidance.

We drift away. Slowly, but surely. But we do not ever drift into holiness.

We do not drift into being a better athlete, lawyer, banker, doctor, businessman or woman, pastor, teacher or professor. And we sure do not drift into being the best fathers and mothers for our children. You will not drift into being a Godly influence as a father, or mother, child or friend.

No, it takes intentional focus and purpose. It takes desire. And as we will see in a moment, it often takes a guardrail to blunt and block our drifting. Intentional focus, purpose, desire: these are words that guard against drifting.

If we examined the consequences of drifting in any sport we enjoy watching – it's finally football season! - or the way we run our businesses, we would see very quickly the potential disasters. Do you want your quarterback drifting his passes into coverage; your base runner drifting off first base; your point guard drifting into a double team; your bookkeeper drifting through your tax returns? Can you imagine your surgeon drifting along through your surgery?

Yet we approach our spiritual lives with a casual, purposeless attitude that we would never tolerate in the *really important* areas of our lives.

I vividly remember, as a child swimming in the ocean in front of our vacation rental house, when my mother would say, "Now you watch this house – it is the blue one - and stay in front of it." The current was normal, or so it seemed. So no big deal. I didn't think a thing about it, and just played and enjoyed myself.

But one minute the house was right in front of me, and the next it moved 300 yards down the beach! What happened? I ... drifted.

Our culture is like a current. At times it is fast and strong, but more often it's deceptively "normal." Either way, it will carry us along and leave us where we did not intend to be.

God knows our tendency to drift, so he warns us about this in his letter to the Hebrews:

> "We must pay more careful attention, therefore, to what
> we have heard, so that we do not drift away."
> (Hebrews 2:1)

GUARDRAILS

We need guardrails in our lives to stop our drifting.

We all need guardrails in our lives to protect from us veering off the safe and wise path, and crashing into a ditch. Guardrails are safety devices we put in place ... purposely. They may be commitments we make with someone to hold us accountable; they may be steps we take to block us from actions that would harm us.

For example, do you think Tiger Woods wishes he had hired someone to protect him from his own instincts and physical drives when it came to the women around him? How much would he have saved if he had paid someone five million dollars a year just to stop him from his affairs with women?

Monetarily he would have saved hundreds of millions of dollars. And emotionally, as well as his reputation, his legacy? No dollar amount could cover his self-destruction. His marriage, his children, even his ability to focus on golf suffered mightily.

A "guardrail" of five million dollars a year to protect himself would have been a bargain!

Guardrails protect us. And the Sabbath is a guardrail given to us from God, a gift, a protective garrison against the attacks from the outside: this culture – and from the inside attacks: our Selfs. We need guardrails against forces that seek to master us.

I like the way Wayne Muller puts it: "Like a path through the forest, Sabbath creates a marker for ourselves so, if we are lost, we can find out way back to our center."

We need protection against forces from without and within, which have the power to overwhelm us. Your Heavenly Father knows this and he obviously knew this from the beginning. Because from the beginning, "In the beginning," he provided the Sabbath as protection from and against the madness of the culture, and the dominance of Self.

Let's take a look at the Sabbath as God's protective guardrail against the invasions of the outside world, and then we will look at the Sabbath as a guardrail against the invasions from within, from our Selfs. Because the barbarians of this culture are at the gate and their attacks are relentless.

BARBARIANS AT THE GATE

Mark Buchanan observes,

> A typical response to threat and burden is to want to flee it. 'If only I could get away" is our mantra. Then I would be safe. Then I could enjoy my life.' But what we find is

that flight becomes captivity: once we begin to flee the things that threaten and burden us, there is no end to the fleeing.

God's solution is surprising. He offers rest. But it's a unique form of rest. It's to rest in him in the midst of our threats and burdens. It's discovering, as David did in seasons of distress, that God is our rock and refuge in the thick of our situation. (*The Rest of God*)

The Sabbath can protect us from the barbarians at the gate, much as a special holiday might. On Christmas and on Thanksgiving I have this feeling of protection from the outside world. Time stops for me. I am at peace. It is warm and comfortable, and safe. Yes, that's it; I feel safe, protected.

No one is calling me, requiring me to perform to their expectations. No one is texting me or emailing me, demanding an immediate response. The barbarians are held at bay, for a day.

It is the same feeling I remember sensing when my daughter was born. That hospital room was like a safe cocoon from the craziness of the outside world. Back then I was in the middle of developing a 400-lot residential development, a fairly stressful and busy time to say the least.

But in the safety of that maternity ward, even my maniacal partners would not dare intrude on that day. You see, when there are thousands of dollars riding on daily decisions, my partners felt they had the right to call me anytime, day or night, week day or weekend. And believe me, Sunday was no exception.

I was on call constantly. But not that day in the hospital, when my daughter was born.

Safe. Protected. No outside intrusions. No outside demands invading my peace. And, don't miss this: no voice in my head saying, "Accomplish something today. Do something."

If I could just recapture that feeling.

Oh, but I can. And so can you, weekly. The Sabbath is a guardrail for you.

Weekly? Is this too much to ever expect in this crazy world in which we live? Not if we follow God's design ... from the beginning ... "In the beginning."

A GARRISON OF PEACE

The Apostle Paul pens a passage in Philippians chapter 4, totally unrelated to keeping the Sabbath. But I am unabashedly applying it anyway, because it paints such a perfect portrait of a "Sabbath to the Lord."

> "Rejoice in the Lord always." God tells is through Paul. "I will say it again: Rejoice! Let your gentleness be evident to all. The Lord is near. Do not be anxious about anything, but in everything, by prayer and petition, with thanksgiving, present your requests to God."

Wouldn't you agree this is a nice start to any Sabbath – rejoice always? And then God's promise:

> "And the peace of God, which transcends all understanding, will ~~guard~~ 'garrison' your hearts and your minds in Christ Jesus." (Philippians 4:4-13 'garrison' added - it is the better translation)

What a promise. Peace – a peace transcending all understanding. Don't you want this peace? Don't we all? As a matter of fact, every decision you make is a quest for peace. You won't necessarily see it this way, but it is just that: A quest for peace.

You buy a new house or new car, a vacation house, switch churches, schools, friends, even divorce your wife or husband, seeking peace. We are all seeking peace, in every decision we make, every action we take.

This may seem overstated, but it is true. Peace, and its accompanying contentment, is what we all want so desperately. We take vacations in search of this peace and contentment. But you are designed and created by God, and his design is the only path to true peace and contentment.

"In the beginning," his design for peace included the Sabbath.

God promises us, "And the peace of God, which transcends all understanding, will guard (garrison) your hearts and your minds in Christ Jesus."

The Greek word for 'guard' is *garrison*. God is promising he will build a garrison around your heart and your mind, protecting his gift of peace, which he will lavish upon you, if you will only trust him.

But what is it we trust about him? We trust he is perfect, and therefore his design is perfect, and therefore his commands are perfect. And we trust that, as the disciple John said, "his commands are not burdensome." (1 John 5:3)

You say you trust God, but you really don't. Oh, you may say you trust that he is perfect, and all-powerful, but when it comes to, "his commands are not burdensome," well, not so much, right? Even more, trusting that he knows what is best for you? We all shipwreck on this one.

We think we actually know what is best for us. We might seek to incorporate some of God's ideas together with ours, but ours are still at the forefront. And when it comes to the Sabbath, we do not just think we know what's best, we *know* we know better.

But can you see how the Sabbath can serve as a protective guard against the mayhem and the invasions of this busy, busy, busy culture? The barbarians are at the gate and you need a garrison of protection.

The Sabbath is God's gift of a garrison to you.

REFUGE – NOT A RESTRICTION

During those times - babies being born, weddings, Christmas, Thanksgiving - time stops, and you are totally free from outside intrusions. You are protected from the invasions of work, from to-do responsibilities, emails, texts, voicemails, and "getting ready" to get ahead for the next workday.

On those days no one is going to get mad at you for not getting a lot of work done. And if they did, you would feel absolutely free of guilt, and even justified in simply responding, "I'm sorry, my child was being born." Or "I'm sorry, I was at my wedding." Or, "I'm sorry, it was Christmas Day." No guilt, no stress.

What if every Sunday could be this way? Imagine your life. Imagine your stress level, your anxiety level, your, "If I don't it, it won't" affliction fading away, defeated. You might never need a vacation.

Most of us take vacations because we *need* to get away. We need a break. We think, "If I could just get away from this daily grind, the stress of all this day-to-day stuff, I could relax and find some peace."

But isn't it true that vacations simply cannot accomplish this for us, at least not until we find true peace in our day-to-day life? A vacation to find peace and quiet, to rest and rejuvenate, is never going to be the solution to this culture of busyness, and our frenetic pace. We must find a garrison of peace in the midst of the mayhem.

With the Sabbath as a refuge, every week, week in and week out, you would not need a vacation away. You would still take vacations, but instead of returning exhausted, as we all are after vacations, you would return refreshed and full of energy, simply because this has become the rhythm of your life.

The Sabbath: God's refuge.

I have a voice constantly in my head saying, "Do something. Accomplish something. Come on Sam, you can't just relax and reflect and enjoy the whole day, one day every week!" This voice use to nag me to the point of my rarely feeling comfortable relaxing and doing nothing - certainly not for a whole day.

But now I can. And so can you. God gives you this gift of a refuge. And being the incredible Father he is, he commands you to embrace his gift of a protective garrison. What a great God: he commands us to take a day off.

What a safe place the Sabbath can be for you. A cocoon, protecting you, nourishing you, surrounding you with comfort and peace. A day, each week – each week! – to step back from the frenetic pace, protected from the madness of the mayhem, by a garrison of peace.

Imagine such a life. Picture your pace slowing, your tension relaxing, your whole body, mind and spirit letting go and loosening up. You can have this. It is real. It is available.

God has given you this gift of a garrison. The barbarians of this lost culture are constantly at the gate, but they cannot penetrate God's garrison of peace, if you will only seek to enter his Sabbath rest.

It is God's desire for you. It is God's plan for you. It is God's commandment to you. And it is God's gift of a Sabbath garrison for you.

The Barbarians from Within

The barbarians of this culture are indeed at the gate, threatening invasion from the outside, but there is another threat seeking to invade from the *inside*: Self. Your Self.

Sabbath Log: Sabbath Week 5

After a few weeks I'm starting to feel protected from the mayhem of our push, push, push culture. This past Sunday that urgent voice in my head kept saying, "For crying out loud, *do* something. Accomplish something!" Instead I just read some more. I read, walked, thought, and reflected.

No TV today. No outside interference of any kind.

A special day. His day. A soft, gentle day.

I am beginning to get a Sabbath groove. And God is right – I like it. (Imagine that)

7

SELF

I HAVE BEEN SINGLE FOR QUITE A WHILE – A LONG TIME, actually. But recently I have realized there is someone in my life who is so important, and might even be that special someone who "completes me." And I want to go public with this.

I think of her constantly. I think she is wonderful, just wonderful. I am totally smitten. I dream about her constantly. She speaks to my heart's desire.

But it's not all positive. As a matter of fact, I'm pretty sure she is holding me back from keeping my entire focus on 721 Ministries. And even though she truly loves the Lord, she is probably, no definitely, getting in the way of my devotion to my Heavenly Father – and my spiritual growth.

If I am objective, I might admit this might not be the healthiest relationship. We have to do what she wants to do all the time. The conversation is always about her. She typically thinks mostly about herself. She is just so full of herself.

The problem is I still think she is so great. I see everything she does in a light most favorable to her. If someone criticizes her, I jump to her defense, even if deep down I know she's wrong. I'll fight to defend her!

She is so funny, so bright, so with it. And she gets me. She understands me. I can always count on her to come to my defense and to whisper in my ear, "They just don't understand you like I do."

Because I am so enraptured with her, I've found myself lying for her, at times even cheating for her. There is practically nothing I wouldn't do for her.

She is like a god to me.

So I protect her at all costs, even when I can look back and see so clearly how she has led me down a path of bad choices, selfish choices, and self-destruction.

Do you want to know her name? She is not really a she: she is ... me. My ... Self.

YOUR TRUE SELF?

(I have re-written this to include you ... your Self)

I think of Self constantly. If I am honest about it, I think of Self all the time. I think Self is wonderful, just wonderful. I am totally smitten with my Self.

But it's not all positive. As a matter of fact I'm pretty sure Self is holding me back from keeping my focus on God. And even though I may truly love the Lord, my Self is probably, no definitely, getting in the way of my devotion to my Heavenly Father – and my spiritual growth.

If I am objective, it might not be the healthiest relationship. We have to do what Self wants to do all the time. The conversation is always about Self. I typically think mostly about Self. I am just so full of Self.

The problem is I think Self is so great. I see everything Self does in a light most favorable to Self. If someone criticizes me, Self jumps to my defense, even if deep down I know Self is wrong. I'll fight to defend Self!

My Self is so funny, so bright, so with it. And Self gets me. Self understands me. I can always count on Self to come to my defense and to whisper in my ear, "They just don't understand you like I do."

Because I am so enraptured with Self, I've found myself lying for Self, at times even cheating for Self. There is practically nothing I wouldn't do for Self.

Self is like a god to me.

So I protect Self at all costs, even when I can look back and see so clearly how Self has led me down a path of bad choices, selfish choices, and self-destruction.

Sound familiar?

YOUR SELF GOD

There is no better way to understand the demanding role of Self in your life than to seek to keep the Sabbath. Keeping the Sabbath will show you exactly who is god in your life – exactly who insists on being in charge.

And it is you ... your Self.

Self is your number one combatant. Self will always seek to draw you away from Jesus and towards yourself. Self wants to be in charge all the time. Self wants to be king! Self will absolutely refuse to surrender to the Sabbath.

Remember, Satan is your enemy. He wants to destroy your soul. If he loses that battle he will spend the rest of your life seeking to ruin your life, to drag you away from the A+ life, and mire you in the C- life. He may try to accomplish this with evil, or he may just settle for average.

My friends at Search Ministries call this "The 3 D's:" Destroy, Distract and Discourage. This is Satan's war strategy. Starting with Adam and Eve, he has employed Self to accomplish his goals.

Think back to his appeal to Adam and Eve: "What, God said to trust him? Don't be ridiculous. You must learn to look after your Selfs. You must learn to trust your Self's instincts, not God's." (Genesis 3)

Satan had such success with this initial strategy, he has kept at it. Think about the egocentric idiots at Babel: "Let's build a tower for our Selfs, so we can enjoy how great we are." (Genesis 11)

Or consider Abraham and Sarah, when they were still childless. God had come the year before and promised them a baby. But oh, come on, it has been a year and what has God done? Nothing. (Genesis 16)

So Satan prods Sarai's Self to speak up, and it sounded a lot like the Garden of Eden: "Abram," Sarai began, "I know God said to trust him, but it's been a year. Don't you think we should take matters into our own hands, and make this happen? If we are going to be happy, maybe we should start trusting our Selfs, and not God."

Or Samson, the poster boy for Self: "I must have that woman for my Self; get her for me." (Judges 14)

And can you just hear Self whispering into King David's ear as he noticed Bathsheba bathing on the roof? "David, you are the King Self. Why should you deny your King Self … anything." (2 Samuel 11)

And then Self's closing gambit: "You deserve it, King David."

Self is Satan's best weapon, and your #1 combatant.

But God gave you the Sabbath as a guardrail to protect you from Self. And you need it. Let's be honest, what has been your first reaction to all this talk so far about the Sabbath?

I know, I know, "Sam is a fanatic!" But after that? Has it been, "Oh boy, I'm going to learn how to please my Heavenly Father more?" Or, "This is so great. This will enhance my focus on God and bring me so much closer. Thank you for helping me to see what I have been so badly missing?"

I doubt it. And don't try to act like it has been. At least not at first. It has been, for every one of us, "How does this affect … *me* … my *Self*?"

Because you are the lead character in the story of your life. You are your own … god.

I'm wrong? I've gone overboard?

WHO IS GOD?

As I have attempted to paint the picture of the Sabbath being a refuge, not a restriction, a gift from God *for* you, to enhance your life, you have thought to your Self: "This is just not realistic. Easy for Sam to say, impossible in my circumstances to actually do."

Now think about that for a moment. What are you, in essence, saying? You are saying God is wrong, and you are right. You are saying God doesn't really understand the complicated life you lead, so *you* must make the necessary adjustments. That makes you ... god.

To probe a tad further: On God's day - Sunday for most of us - how much time do you actually give God? If you are a churchgoer, maybe about 2 hours: 10:00 to 12:00? And really, because of all the socializing and distractions at church, how much of that time does he actually get - maybe 20%?

After that it's, "Whew, I got that over with. Now I can get back to doing what *I* want to do."

I have to admit, I have always been a bit suspicious of those who go to the 'early church' service: "Let's get the church thing out of the way early so we can have the whole day to our ... Selfs!"

Seeking to keep the Sabbath will cure any illusions you have about who wants to be the god in your life. Your Heavenly Father obviously foresaw what a combatant Self was going to be. So he introduced the Sabbath, in part to give us at least one day off from trying to be god.

TRUST AND SURRENDER

And, as with everything in your spiritual journey with the Lord, it boils down to trust and surrender. Trust and surrender is always the core issue. The entire Biblical story emphasizes Trust and Surrender.

And so it is with keeping the Sabbath.

When you seek to keep the Sabbath, you will run into the wall of Self. Trust Self, or trust God. Surrender to Self, and what Self wants to do ... all the time! ... or surrender to God, and his way.

Just as with tithing, the issue is not money, it is your trust. God says to you, "Just trust me in this: give me 10% of your income and I will do more in your life with the remaining 90% than you could ever do by holding onto the full 100%."

The currency in tithing appears to be money, but it's actually trust and surrender. The currency of Sabbath-keeping appears to be time, but again, it is trust and surrender.

Think about this little math exercise:

In each week there are 7 days with 24 hours = 168 hours. But you're only awake, say 16 hours of those days, so 7 days x 16 hours =112 hours waking hours.

Now, if you were to observe the Sabbath, just for your daylight hours of each Sunday, that would be, say twelve hours. (Of course the Jews considered the Sabbath to be twenty-four hours, starting the night before and running till sundown. But I am setting my expectations low here)

If we divide 12 waking hours a day into 112 waking hours a week, we get about 10%. So if you actually gave these daylight hours each Sunday to the Lord, this would equal 10%. A coincidence?

JUST ONE DAY?

Just as with monetary tithing, the currency of the Sabbath is Trust and Surrender. Will you surrender being the god of your life for one day? Or will your Self continue to insist on being god all seven days?

As I mentioned before, when I first introduced this Sabbath idea to the men's groups with whom I meet each week, a few of the men said, "But every day should be a Sabbath to the Lord. After Jesus came, we are no longer - and should no longer be – bound to just one day."

To which I say, "Absolutely, that would be so nice. But no one is actually doing it. So let's start with trying to set aside just one day *to* the Lord, and away *from* Self."

God's promise for seeking to follow his design in keeping the Sabbath is to lavish your life with joy and peace and energy and clarity and … contentment. His plan is for your one Sabbath day to then begin to overflow into the other six days with the same joy, peace, and contentment.

I do not know precisely how he will do this, but through the power of the Holy Spirit I know he will. Over the years I have learned that trusting and surrendering to my Self has always, every single time, been a bad trade. But trusting and surrendering to God's design, has every time, without fail, brought "streams of living water overflowing from within." (John 7:38)

I love the way C.S. Lewis chides us about Self, and wanting to be our own gods:

> "We must not think pride is something God forbids because he is offended at it, or that humility is something he demands as due to his own dignity – as if God himself was proud. He is not in the least worried about his dignity. The point is, he wants you to know him: wants to give you himself. And he and you are two things of such a kind that if you really get into any kind of touch with him you will, in fact, be humble – delightfully humble, feeling the infinite relief of for once having got rid of all the silly nonsense about your own dignity which has made you restless and unhappy all your life.
>
> He is trying to make you humble in order to make this moment possible: trying to take off a lot of silly, ugly, fancy-dress in which we have all got ourselves up and are strutting about like the little idiots we are. I wish I had got a bit further with humility myself: if I had, I could probably tell you more about the relief, the comfort, of taking the fancy-dress off – getting rid of the false

self, with all its 'Look at me' and 'Aren't I a good boy?' and all its posing and posturing. To get even near it, even for a moment, is like a drink of cold water to a man in a desert." (*Mere Christianity*)

SABBATH LOG: SABBATH WEEK 6

I had brunch today after speaking at a church service. I didn't really want to, being an introvert, I was ready to get home to be by myself. But it was clear this was a "Relationship over Rules" scenario, so I did. At the service that morning another preacher was in attendance. We bumped into him and his friends at the brunch.

I had mentioned in my talk about my attention to the Sabbath, so later this preacher, for whom I have much respect, said to his friend, "If Sam was really serious about keeping the Sabbath he wouldn't be out having brunch today."

Of course, he was out having brunch, too. But it did give me the opportunity to relate to my friend about relationship over rules.

All in all, brunch was the right thing to do, for relationship. But as I am now in my fifth week of this Sabbath journey, I was acutely aware that I could be treating the Sabbath just like everyone else.

8

RHYTHMS

"The Sabbath gives us an opportunity to weave rest not only into our schedules but into the fabric of our souls."

—Darrin Patrick

*"Are you tired? Worn out? Burned out on religion? Come to me. Get away with me and you'll recover your life. I'll show you how to take a real rest. Walk with me and work with me — watch how I do it. **Learn the unforced rhythms of grace.** I won't lay anything heavy or ill-fitting on you. Keep company with me and you'll learn to live freely and lightly."*

—Matthew 11:28-30, The Message, Bold Added

LEARN THE UNFORCED RHYTHMS OF GRACE

WE HAVE DAYS BECAUSE THE EARTH ROTATES IN TWENTY-four hours. We have months because the moon revolves around the earth. We have years because the earth revolves around the sun. But why do we have seven-day weeks? There is no scientific or natural reason.

God set it up this way. For a reason. For a rhythm.

God is all about rhythms.

The whole world operates on a weekly calendar designed and ordained by a God many do not know, and some even despise. During the French Revolution the people sought to do away with both the crown and the church, so they put in place a 10-day week, in part to eliminate the Sabbath. During the Communist revolution a 5-day week was instituted for much the same reason.

Neither worked. They could not possibly. They were out of God's rhythm.

Why did God give us a seven-day week?

God is all about rhythm.

From the solar systems to the seasons, even to your heartbeat, everything about our world, and even our bodies, is rhythmic. And everything about our world flows better and much easier when things are in rhythm. Including your life.

Oswald Chambers captures perfectly the picture of a life flowing in rhythm with your Maker:

> "A Christian is someone who trusts in the knowledge and the wisdom of God, not in his own abilities. If we have a purpose of our own, it destroys the simplicity and the calm, relaxed pace which should be characteristic of the children of God." *My Utmost For His Highest* August 5

"... the simplicity and the calm, relaxed pace ...." Should this be characteristic of a child of God? Do you have this? I doubt it. It is close to impossible to find this, and then to hold onto it in our weekly day-to-day rushed routines.

Notice there is a pace here; no one is advocating sitting in a closet and expecting God to run your life for you. Yet it is a calm, relaxed pace. But we ignore God's invitation to a life of relaxed pace, and instead, without thinking about what we are doing, we conform to the culture's pull. Just as God warns,

"Do not conform to the pattern of this world, but be transformed by the renewing of your mind. Then you will know what God's will is—his good, pleasing and perfect will." (Romans 12:2)

GOD GUIDES – SATAN RUSHES

The "patterns of this world" have no rhythm. The patterns of this world are all about rushing to and from. Remember: God guides; Satan rushes.

So stop. Cease. "Sabbath" means "to cease."

Stop conforming to the patterns of this world. This world's patterns are like the rushing whitewater rapids: fast, rocky and shallow. But God's pace is like the still water of a slow river: Still water runs deep. Renew your mind by seeking to find God's calm, relaxed, rhythmic pace.

For the past few months I have been going to a Zumba class on Tuesday nights. I love it! At first, with absolutely zero white boy rhythm, it was pure exercise: great exercise, but all work, no play. Now that I'm getting the rhythm, the exercise has become dance, or at least Sam's version of dance.

Now I'm having fun and the sixty minutes fly by. It is just so much easier and so much more enjoyable flowing with the rhythm.

Too many of us live Monday through Monday through Monday through Monday: weeks turning into months into years into decades. Can you relate? There can be no A+ Life there. Our weekly routines are numbing. Like my first experiences at Zumba: all herky-jerky work. No rhythm.

But from the beginning God gave us a unique rhythm: Monday, Tuesday, Wednesday, Thursday, Friday, Saturday, stop.

Stop.

Rest. Reflect. Rejuvenate. Set apart. Listen. Revere. Rhythm.

The Sabbath creates an ebb and flow for your week. For six days accomplish, go, get it done, achieve – the seventh day, stop. Breathe. Reflect. Listen.

Stop. Get your groove back.

You see, deep inside you know you need a rhythm to your life. But our culture has robbed us of any semblance of a balanced, rhythmic life. Consequently, we are not even consciously aware of this need. But we know something is missing, something is out of whack.

So we try a glass of wine … or two? … each night. We try smoking pot, yoga, exercise, fishing, hunting, sports, reading, anything to stop the madness of our out-of-balance lives. Anything to recapture this sense of rhythm God designed in you.

These things we try are not all necessarily bad, by themselves, but they will never be able to recapture what we are missing. They might assist, but they simply cannot replace God's original design for rhythm. He designed the Sabbath to give us this rhythm to our weeks, so we could recapture it for our lives.

And if we capture his rhythmic pace, it will filter throughout our entire life: day to day, week to week, year to year.

WORSHIP

I try to worship God every day of the week. I think I do a pretty good job, too. At least a lot better than most of you! And since God grades on the curve – he doesn't?? – I'm obviously better off than you.

All kidding aside, I do try to worship God, to worship and adore my Savior Jesus, every day of the week. But since this Sabbath journey started for me, I can see just how much I need a day set apart to worship. The Sabbath pulls together all my week-day worships, and gives them a rhythm.

As Eugene Peterson writes,

"Worship is the primary way in which the people of God stay in rhythm with their creation, find their place in creation, who they are and where they come from, internalizing the creation cadences of God who made heaven and earth, who said, "Let there be light," who created male and female, who said "be fruitful and

multiply, and fill the earth and subdue it," who saw everything he had made and behold, it was very good,"
who rested and sanctified the seventh day.

"Our text is unequivocal: Remember and observe
this Sabbath day; take the Genesis week into your lives
in this grand practice of contemplation; get creation into
your nervous system ..." (Eugene Peterson, *Christ Plays
In Ten Thousand Places*)

I have found I need this day set apart, to set apart my life into a
rhythm of God's design. The Sabbath has become the glue that binds
my other six days together into a rhythm I simply cannot produce
on my own.

ROUTINES INTO RHYTHMS

Monday to Monday living, or probably more applicable for most of
us, weekend to weekend living, will not get our grooves back. We
need a day ... off ... set apart. We need a day to stop. We need a day
to regain our balance, our footing, our sense of place.

We need a day to stop and regain our rhythm.

We do not want to be living a life of just mowing the lawn. Just
maintaining, just keeping the grass cut. Or like an endless shower
cycle of rinse and repeat, rinse and repeat.

"It's all about pausing and connecting with God without
the distracting chaos of our everyday routines. For one
day a week, we step out of the fray and let God direct
our day according to His rhythm, not ours.

"God's rhythm preserves a space in us to hear His
voice, reveals the places we're off track, and prevents us
from being filled with unnecessary clutter. Quiet rest al-
lows us to see the places where we're going our own
way, the areas where we're more self-pleasing than
God-pleasing, the idle words that need to be reined in.

During the down time, we can deal with the mental clutter and focus on the ways of God.

"The Sabbath makes this possible.

"Taking one day for rest gives my soul the freedom it so desperately needs. Freedom to breathe. Space to breathe. Inhaling and exhaling in a gentle rhythm set by God." (*Space to Exhale*, Lysa TerKeurst)

The Sabbath became both a rhythm breaker and rhythm setter for me during this journey. I started by changing my routine into a rhythm. I did this mostly by just deciding to shift my perspective. Then God, as he so often wonderfully does, turned my changing into his *transforming*.

Let me repeat that because it is vitally important: To create a rhythm, I simply made the decision to do so. Then God came in and transformed my feeble attempt to change into transformation. I did this by viewing my weekly routine through a different lens. At first it felt unnatural, kind of silly, actually.

I felt like I was trying to create a soundtrack to my week. You know, like watching a movie of me, going through my routine, but with rhythmic music in the background.

It reminds me of what Eugene Peterson wrote as a Commentary in his *The Message Study Bible*:

"If the moments of your day-to-day life were recorded as musical notes, what kind of music would they make? Would they sound like a breezy pop song or hard-driving rap music? Or would they sound like a beautiful symphony with structured pauses that give resonance to the notes?"

So I just kept reminding myself, "Today is Monday, workout day with BoBo. Today is Tuesday; it's Zumba night. Today is Wednesday, lunch with Irv after the 721 Meeting." These parts then began to make up the rhythm for the week.

And it worked! Or I should say God honored my attempts to get into rhythm with him. This is what He does so graciously. He takes our very human, very limited attempts to please him, to follow him, and he transforms them into something special.

Each of us has a weekly routine of some sort. We eat meals, we work out, we have various work activities, as well as social activities each week. My Zumba class has become part of my weekly workout rhythm. Although you might call it my weekly workout routine, I call it my weekly rhythm.

On Tuesdays I have a pattern. On Wednesdays I eat and fellowship with my friend, Irv. It's a mid-week part of the flow of my week. As with my newfound rhythm in my Zumba class, my weeks are becoming easier and more enjoyable as my routine becomes a rhythm.

I feel like I am drafting behind God, being pulled by his power, as a cyclist does in races.

My cyclist friends espouse the benefits of getting behind another rider and drafting off his windstream. They say it is much easier and requires much less effort to draft off the power from his windstream.

And so it is with your Heavenly Father. Get into his rhythm and draft behind his power.

Light a Candle

On Friday evenings I stop, and breathe … deeply. I light a candle. Go ahead, laugh at me. I am very comfortable in my manhood. I light a candle. I breathe deeply.

I stop.

The candle on Friday nights is a seemingly minor thing. But for me it is a big thing. It is a signal. A reminder: "It's Friday, Sam. Breathe. Relax. Recoup. Reflect on what you have accomplished this week; and not on what you did not get done."

I try to avoid all socializing on Friday nights, because it throws off this rhythm. And I light a candle again on Sunday mornings. I light a candle. I breathe deeply. I listen for God. I let the grace of God flow over me. I feel his presence, his peace, his power. His rhythm.

Oh, I try to do this throughout the week, but it is not the same as my Friday/Sunday rhythm.

Again, Jesus painted the perfect portrait of this rhythm when he invited us to draft behind him:

> "Come to me. Get away with me and you'll recover your life. I'll show you how to take a real rest. Keep company with me and you'll learn to live freely and lightly. **Learn the unforced rhythms of grace."** (Matthew 11:28-30, The Message)

"The unforced rhythms of grace." Breathe this in. Let these unforced rhythms of grace flow over you. Start with next Sunday, and light a candle. Breathe … deeply. Reflect. Relax. Listen for God to speak to you. He is real. He will.

If you recall, God commanded us to " Keep the Sabbath holy" – "holy" meaning to be set apart. So from a purely practical approach here are a few tips on how to "set apart" your routine days into rhythm days.

Create a rhythm by setting apart two or three mornings a week for a walk, or a special morning hot drink. Maybe you could choose a particular morning to sit outside while you read scripture and pray.

You could do the same with your evenings. They do not have to all be the same, you know. Listen to music with your favorite person on a Wednesday night, while you sip a glass of your favorite beverage. Pick a day a week to have lunch with someone, each week.

Choose a day to walk with your spouse, or your children. Change your workout routines, even your hobby routines. Set days apart for a different way of doing the same old thing. Now I know this will be a radical idea, but perhaps you could set a time during the week to have some … silence.

Here are a few other ways suggested by the "Sabbath Manifesto" (http://www.sabbathmanifesto.org/) to set apart your routine and create a rhythm:

SABBATH MANIFESTO

Avoid Technology	Connect with Loved ones
Nurture your health	Get outside
Avoid commerce	Light candles
Drink wine	Eat bread
Find silence	Give back

I may be doing a poor job of articulating this idea of rhythm, but God set up our world with a rhythm from the very beginning. So my advice is to talk to him about it. Ask him why he set up a seven-day week, and then asked (commanded, actually) us to stop on that seventh day. Ask him to help you find his rhythm. He is real; he will respond.

SABBATH LOG: SABBATH WEEK 7

Today my dear friend Billy asked me, for the umpteenth time, to come watch his daughter's soccer team. They play every Sunday somewhere, because travel ball plays somewhere every weekend. Can there be a more startling indictment of losing the Sabbath, not to mention any semblance of rest, relaxation and recovery, than travel ball?

But I went, and what I saw shocked me. Hundreds of families were spread over this vast county soccer complex. They were set up for tailgating and watching soccer. I am not saying these were bad people, but I am saying my heart was broken for just how blind they were to any idea of setting this day apart, and how they were missing any idea that their family needed some downtime... some together time.

Over these years of doing 721 Ministries, we have seen countless families going different places: each weekend the mom goes in one direction with the daughters, and the dad goes elsewhere with the sons.

Argh!

No rhythm, no rest no way to rejuvenate, no recovery.

9

DELIGHT

"The Sabbath is the link between the paradise which has passed away and the paradise which is yet to come."

—Andrew Wylie

THE BIG CHILL: DELIGHT

THERE IS A SCENE IN *THE BIG CHILL* WHERE SARAH (GLENN Close) and her husband, Harold, (Kevin Kline) are in the kitchen chatting with their best friend, Meg (Mary Kay Place). Harold is on the phone with their young daughter, Molly. Toward the end of the conversation Molly apparently asks Harold to hand the phone off, and as he does, the mom, Sarah, steps forward, naturally assuming Molly wants to talk to her.

But it is their friend Meg to whom Molly wants to talk. As Meg takes the phone, her face lights up, and a big, warm smile spreads across her face. We can sense the same smile from Molly. Their conversation is precious, absolutely precious. It is obvious the two love each other, and have such a special place in each other's lives.

Pure joy. They ... delight ... in each other.

God gives us two insights into this kind of delight, and the promises linked to these delights are nothing short of astounding.

He promises that if you will delight in him, he will give you the desires of your heart.

And, he wants you to delight in his Sabbath gift to you. (Isaiah 58:13-14) His promise is a life permeated with joy, fullness, energy, clarity, creativity, and power ... nothing short of the A+ Life that is truly life.

Delight in the Sabbath? How to do this, when most of us still consider the Sabbath commandment a meddling restriction on our freedom to do whatever we want, whenever we want?

The answer is found in our bond with the Lord. We must first find our delight in the Lord, before we will ever find his Sabbath to be a delight.

> "Delight yourself in the LORD and he will give you the
> desires of your heart." (Psalm 37:4)

THE DESIRES OF YOUR HEART

What do you think the delights of your heart are? I bet you could put together a list quickly, couldn't you? Your list would include material things, along with emotional and relational desires, as well. Some would be sincere and heart-felt, even altruistic, others purely self-serving.

So would mine. But ... do not miss this: they would all be *your* desires.

What I have learned over all these years walking with Jesus, is I do not have a clue what the true desires of my heart are. He does. I do not.

Oh, I've been very sure I did know, and therefore did everything in my power to obtain these desires. But more often than not, I was wrong. Now I see that what God is saying is, "Sam, take your focus off what you think you desire, and place it on me. My promise to you is if you will do this, you will turn around one day, sooner than later, and you will indeed have the true desires of your heart.

Because I will give them to you. And you will be the most surprised person on the planet."

ANAG

"Delight in me," God says. I am learning to do this, and his promise is absolutely true.

A typical definition of delight is:

1. a high degree of pleasure or enjoyment; joy; rapture: *She takes great delight in her job.*
2. something that gives great pleasure: *The dance was a delight to see.* (Dictionary.com)

And this is typically the Hebrew meaning behind "delight" when used throughout the Older Testament. But in Psalm 37:4 a different, unique word is employed, to paint the picture of a different, unique relationship.

The Hebrew word is "Anag" and its meaning might surprise you:

> "**Anag**": delicate – luxurious   e.g. A garment: Silk - "Take delight in, simply for what it is" (Strong's Complete Dictionary)

The picture is one of someone admiring an object just because of its individual beauty. Imagine a woman rubbing an Egyptian silk scarf across her face, relishing its delicate, luxurious feel. She delights in the scarf for no other reason than it is … a pure delight to her senses.

And this is what God means by "Delighting yourself in him." Not for what he can do for you, but simply because he is such a wonderfully pure delight.

Do you have someone in your life who is a pure delight?

Grandchildren are a pure delight. Or maybe you have a grand-parent like this. Or someone who is special to you, in a most special way. Now picture a day celebrating them. Your granddaughter's birthday; your father's 80th birthday. Or even your wedding anniversary.

This day is a celebration, a delight, not because of the day, but because of the *person* in whom you take such delight. The day, the event, may be fun and wonderful. It may even be a gloriously good time. But we have all had good times at parties and events. Good times are not the delights we are talking about here.

The day is so special, set apart even, because your delight is in that special person. And this delight overflows and washes across the day, making the day a delight in itself. But only because your wife, or husband, or grandchild or friend is such a delight to you.

My daughter and I go to New York once a year. The trip is a pure delight for me. I have been to New York without her other times and I always enjoy myself. But it is only a *delight* when I go with Britton. New York City is not the delight; it is the person with me, my precious daughter, in whom I delight.

Could this be what God wants for us, for our Sabbaths? Could he want us to so delight in him, we naturally delight in his day?

It certainly seems so as we read his invitation and promise in Isaiah:

> "If you keep your feet from breaking the Sabbath and
> from doing as you please on my holy day, **if you call
> the Sabbath a delight** and the Lord's holy day honora-
> ble,
> and if you honor it by not going your own way and not
> doing as you please or speaking idle words,
> 14 then you will find your joy in the Lord, and I will
> cause you to ride in triumph on the heights of the land
> and to feast on the inheritance of your father Jacob."
> For the mouth of the Lord has spoken. (Isaiah 58:13-14,
> bold added)

DOING AS YOU PLEASE – TWICE!

The invitation:

Did you notice how many times God warns us to get away from that constant combatant, *Self,* which we discussed in Chapter 7? "Stop "doing as *you* please on my holy day;" stop "going *your own* way;" and again, twice, in case we missed it: stop "doing as *you* please or speaking idle words."

Please do not miss God repeating, "Not doing as you please," twice, and also including "going your own way" as a third emphasis. This is one of my two guiding principles in my Sabbath quest:

1. To – From
2. Am I just doing as I please?

I may go to lunch or dinner on a Sunday, or I may go to a movie, but not without at least thinking about it. Not without at least discussing it with Jesus. Not without a sense of peace about it. (A true sense of peace, not an uncertain sense of peace from my great ability to rationalize!)

I am now asking myself, "Is this doing as I please?" And if the answer is anywhere near, "Yes," then I will not do it.

In essence, God is inviting us to get over our Selves, to take a day to not be the #1 focus of our lives, and open up to something bigger than us: "… my holy day."

The promise:

" … then you will find your joy in the LORD."

That would be enough, wouldn't it? To find *joy*? I want that, don't you – a life overflowing with joy??

Yet God sweetens the pot with promises I confess are too immense for me to wrap my head around. But knowing the vast and outlandishly lavish way of God, I feel confident he means this promise to be over the top:

> " ...and I will cause you to ride in triumph on the heights of the land and to feast on the inheritance of your father Jacob."

Here is how Eugene Peterson translates this Isaiah passage:

> If you watch your step on the Sabbath and don't use my holy day for personal advantage, If you treat the Sabbath as a day of joy, GOD's holy day as a celebration, If you honor it by refusing 'business as usual,' making money, running here and there— Then you'll be free to enjoy GOD! Oh, I'll make you ride high and soar above it all. I'll make you feast on the inheritance of your ancestor Jacob." Yes! GOD says so." (The Message)

This reminds me of God's promises about "soaring like eagles with wings" in Isaiah 40:31:

> " ...but those who hope in the LORD will renew their strength. They will soar on wings like eagles; they will run and not grow weary, they will walk and not be faint."

And do not miss the "feast on the inheritance" part, either. God promises his Sabbath will become a feast for you. A feast! Growing up we had Sunday dinner (that's Sunday lunch in the South) every Sunday at my Grandmother McLeod's home. Venetia, the cook, made the best macaroni and cheese in the universe.

Every Sunday dinner was a small feast. I can still smell her macaroni and cheese, her rice and gravy, and her fried chicken. What a delight! Yet God ups the ante. He promises the entire day, and then your life, will become a feast for you.

"Soaring and feasting." But how? We must first delight in this Heavenly Father who makes these lavish promises and then we will find delight in his day.

A FEAST OF FRIENDS

Just as we do with our favorite friends.

A friend who is a pure delight would be someone with whom you feel totally safe, with no judging and no negative vibes. They would have no hidden agendas. Transparency comes easily between the two of you, and you can laugh at yourselves with each other. You both know what is important to the other, and so it is important to you.

Fun and positive, and pure joy is how you feel about this relationship.

Your children know this person is a delight to you, as well, and so they share in your delight: like Meg and Molly in *The Big Chill*. My daughter knows which friends are my oldest and best friends. She can sense the friends who bring me such joy. So she naturally finds the same joy in them.

Is there any chance your children, or those close to you, would ever sense a Big Chill, Meg and Molly bond of delight, when you talk about Jesus?

Oh my. Imagine if they did. Imagine the generational influence.

Could your child ever say, "I don't know who Dad is talking to, but I can tell he's talking about the Lord, because he's in such a delightful mood."

Now ponder this: Do you feel this way about Jesus? When you think of Jesus do you think, "What a great friend and Savior; I can't believe my good fortune, having him in my life? He is all positive, always supporting me, never condemning me. He's always on my side – always for me, with me, and before me. And he's fun to be with! Jesus is a ... delight to me."

You can have this. This is real, and this is obtainable. Yes, you can actually live this. Jesus can be a positive delight in your life.

Here is the progression: Delight in the Lord – Delight in his Word – Delight in his Commands – Delight in his Sabbath.

It is the key to the true richness of the Kingdom, and it is the key to a rich Sabbath life.

As you see Jesus for the delight he absolutely is, you will see his Father for the delight he truly is, and you will be on the path to delighting in his Sabbath.

SABBATH LOG: SABBATH WEEK 8

Today I spoke at another church. I will admit I do not know how to reconcile the work of speaking at churches on Sundays, but I do know I now get home as fast as I can for the silence and solitude of my home, alone.

These seven weeks of my Sabbath journey have instilled in me a strong desire for silence and solitude, as well as an aversion to busyness, or chatting with others about news, weather and sports. Or TV.

The gift of the Sabbath has indeed become a refuge, no longer a restriction. God is changing my heart and opening my eyes to the riches of his plan for Sabbath rest. This reminds me of a favorite passage:

> I pray that the eyes of your heart may be enlightened in order that you may know the hope to which he has called you, the riches of his glorious inheritance in his holy people, [19] and his incomparably great power for us who believe. (Ephesians 1:18-19)

10

SABBATH REST

"I know Sabbath is more than just rest, a self-induced time-out from the world. I also believe that if the Lord created something, modeled it and commanded it, I should probably pay close attention."

—Kristen Schell

I NEED MORE REST. YOU NEED MORE REST. OUR CULTURE needs more rest. But wait, what a wimpy thing to be talking about: rest. "Lunch is for wimps!" and all that bluster.

I love to take naps. My friends don't say it, but they think I'm lazy. But I see them carrying around their cups of caffeine hits, like an intravenous life support hooked up to their bodies, delivering that all-important energy.

Naps are not for wimps. Rest is not for wimps. Do not fall for that nonsense.

Satan loves to keep you busy and pressing and stressing. Let's imagine one of Satan's weekly sales meetings. He has some young demons sitting around the conference table and he asks them what their strategy is for the coming week.

The first proudly says, "I plan to entice my young man into a drug addiction."

Satan responds, "Well that's okay, but we don't actually get that many souls using that technique, and when we do, often they end up turning back to God, as they realize the failure of their ways, and their desperate need for a Savior."

The next demon smirks, and announces, "I've got my girl on the verge of an affair. She doesn't see it coming, but I've got her having lunch with a coworker, and we know this is how we typically get affairs started."

Satan grimaces and observes, "But it is often the same outcome. Sure, I know it is great fun to wreak such havoc, but if you really want to have long-term success, you will just slowly suck them into the world of busyness and constant motion. That is more subtle, and lasting, and we have captured many a soul with this simple strategy."

Then Satan exclaims, "Always remember our motto: If you can't make them bad, make them busy!"

RECOVER

But your loving Heavenly Father says, "No, take a rest. I love you. I want you to have the A+ Life" – "Life to the full," as Jesus says.

Rest is not a luxury, it is an essential. Any personal fitness trainer will advise you to take time to allow your body to rest and recover. I have even heard the motto, "Get stronger on the sofa." When we push our bodies, through constant and unceasing training, we will likely burn them out, and break them down.

With no recovery time, our muscles will mutiny on us, breaking down, rather than growing stronger. Our resting time, in the midst of weight training, is just as important as our working out time. "Get stronger on the sofa!" And so it is with our body-mind-spirits. We need a rest. We need to refresh. The Sabbath is rest for the soul.

But we keep charging ahead. The Energy Drink industry has exploded. Total sales in 2010 were 4 billion, leaping to 12 billion in 2011. And here's a telling statistic: in 2012, sales for the New 5-Hour

Energy "Extra Strength" drink were up 744% over the original 5-Hour Energy.

5 Hour Energy is no longer enough – we need Extra Strength Energy for crying out loud!

And this is precisely what this energy drink addiction is all about: we are indeed *crying out loud*: "I need rest, I need energy, but I don't know where to find it." You can only find this rest in the safe arms of your Heavenly Father. Deep rest. Soul rest.

REM SOUL REST

As Augustine puts it: "Thou hast made us for thyself, O Lord, and our heart is restless until it finds its rest in thee." (Augustine of Hippo, *The Confessions of Saint Augustine*)

Jesus gives us an astonishing invitation to this rest:

> "Come to me, all you who are weary and burdened, and
> I will give you rest. Take my yoke upon you and learn
> from me, for I am gentle and humble in heart, and you
> will find rest for your souls." (Matthew 11:28-30)

"I will give you rest – rest for your souls." This is what you and I need: soul rest. Deep REM soul rest. The kind of rest that penetrates so deeply it shapes your entire perspective on life. We are all searching for this soul rest, because our souls are "restless until it finds its rest in thee."

We are exhausted, physically, mentally, and emotionally. So we turn to energy drinks of all kinds –some with alcohol and some just caffeine and sugar. And for the latest generation, a combination of both.

We crave rest, we crave peace. Come on, you know I'm right. You need soul rest. Too many try to find this rest by getting away, escaping by vacation to a restful place. But as soon as we re-enter our crazy day-to-day world any rest we tried to capture is lost ... almost immediately.

Ugh. That is the epitome of the C- life.

The kind of rest to which Jesus invites you will not disappear the moment you re-enter the cultural mayhem of your day-to-day life. In fact, the kind of rest Jesus offers doesn't require an exit at all.

> "Peace I leave with you; my peace I give you. I do not give to you as the world gives." (John 14:27)

Jesus' peace penetrates so deeply that you carry it with you at all times. I have found in my Sabbath journey the gate to this soul rest. It is setting apart the Sabbath. Now with full confession, I had found much of this soul rest before I embarked on this Sabbath discovery expedition. Walking with Jesus daily, "In a conversational walk through life, talking with God about what we are doing together," will infuse this kind of soul rest. (Dallas Willard)

But it wasn't until I stepped through the gate of Sabbath surrender – surrendering my day and my way, to his way, his day – that I truly began to see and sense this pervasive soul rest.

Jesus calls out, "… and you will find rest for your souls."

Isaiah, seven hundred years before, calls out the same invitation:

> "…then you will find your joy in the Lord, and I will cause you to ride in triumph on the heights of the land and to feast on the inheritance of your father Jacob." (Isaiah 58:14)

"Finding your joy in the LORD, riding in triumph on the heights of the land, feasting on your inheritance from your heavenly Father," this is what soul rest looks like.

For most of my life, at least until I was born again at thirty-eight, and even for several years after that, I sought to find my joy in Sam, and I rode in triumph on Sam's accomplishments, and I feasted in many a fine restaurant. Yet, I was … exhausted … constantly.

But to the outside world I would have appeared full of energy and purpose. Yet inwardly, in my limping-along soul, I was simply exhausted. How could I not be? I was running on the cultural fuel, powered by multiple cups of coffee a day, a drink or two, or three, every night (just to rest and relax).

Jesus came along and said, "Come on Sam, you think this is the A+ life? Follow me, come to me, and I will show you a life with just as many accomplishments, but with a soul rest that will render all these dysfunctional coping mechanisms of yours unnecessary."

I did follow, and he did show me his soul rest.

Rest, renewal, recovery and rejuvenation all take time ... still time ... *being still* time. I hope you can find this rest during your Monday – Saturday life, but I doubt you will be able to get past a mere surface rest until you first find real rest in your Sabbaths. God seems to have set the Sabbath as the gateway into his REM soul rest.

ABANDON THE OUTCOME TO GOD

Rest, and the Sabbath, is all about trust – trusting God at his word:

> "For the pagans run after all these things, and your heavenly Father knows that you need them. But seek first the Kingdom of God and his righteousness, and all these things will be given to you as well."
> (Matthew 6:32-33)

"All these things" are what our 24/7 culture is chasing. "All these things" are what you think you must have, and so you must grab them for yourself, and you must then hold onto them tightly for fear of losing them. Because without them you simply cannot be happy.

And so you lose the life you were so desperately trying to save, and miss the life Jesus invites you to find:

> "For whoever wants to save his life will lose it, but who-ever loses his life for me will find it. 26 What good will it be for a man if he gains the whole world, yet forfeits

his soul? Or what can a man give in exchange for his soul." (Matthew 16:25-26)

This whole fruitless, chasing after exercise leaves you exhausted. But God promises *all these things* will be taken care of ... if you trust him. That is a bold promise, and one not to be ignored.

What would this trust look like in our frenetic world? Would we sit in a closet praying, and expect him to take care of everything? No. We would actively pursue our purpose in life. We could be competitive, even proactive and aggressive in our business. Nowhere in scripture do we see God promoting laziness.

But, and do not miss this all-important but, after all our effort, we would feel safe in "abandoning the outcome to God."

Abandoning the outcome to God is a sign of soul rest. Abandoning the outcome to God is the key to soul rest. And it is one of the hardest things for us to do. Abandoning the outcome to God is all about trusting that God will always deliver the best outcome.

This is why honoring the Sabbath, especially not working to get ahead, will require us to abandon the outcome to God. Most of us think that if we do not work harder to control the outcome we are being irresponsible.

We do not control the outcome, but so much of our exhaustion comes from trying so desperately to do so. If you are going to honor the Sabbath, to set it apart, especially if you are one of those "If I don't it won't" people, then you will have to learn to abandon the outcome to God.

The freedom you will experience will be life changing. Not just for you, but for everyone around you.

11

REMEMBER

"*If we take care of the moments, the years will take care of themselves.*"

—Eugene Peterson

"*When they went across the lake, the disciples forgot to take bread.* ⁶ "*Be careful," Jesus said to them. "Be on your guard against the yeast of the Pharisees and Sadducees." ⁷ They discussed this among themselves and said, "It is because we didn't bring any bread." ⁸ Aware of their discussion, Jesus asked, "You of little faith, why are you talking among yourselves about having no bread? ⁹ Do you still not understand? **Don't you remember** the five loaves for the five thousand, and how many basketfuls you gathered, or the seven loaves for the 4000 ...?"*

—Matthew 16: 5-9 bold added

FTER FEEDING THE FOUR THOUSAND JESUS CHIDES THE disciples, "Don't you remember?" Throughout the Bible we see God reminding us of who he is and what he has already, and always done for us.

The book of Deuteronomy is all about Moses reminding the Israelites about what God has done for them. Joshua then reminds the Israelites to always remind their children what God has done for them:

> "And Joshua set up at Gilgal the twelve stones they had taken out of the Jordan. ²¹ He said to the Israelites, "In the future when your descendants ask their fathers, 'What do these stones mean?' ²² tell them, 'Israel crossed the Jordan on dry ground.' ²³ For the LORD your God dried up the Jordan before you until you had crossed over." (Joshua 4:20-23)

The Psalms are full of "Remembers." As a matter of fact, God reminds us to "remember" over two hundred times. I wonder why?

We need to be reminded, and we need to remember, often, what God has done for us, and how powerfully perfect and perfectly loving he is. We are weak, fragile humans, and we forget so easily our experiences with God. In times of stress and anxiety, the many examples of God's direct involvement in our lives seem to fly out of our minds, and we feel we are isolated and on our own.

And even when we do remember, our doubt still wavers, and we wonder, "But will he be there for me … this time?"

Recall in Chapter 3: The Sabbath Commandments, God reminded his people how much he had already done for them before he gave them the Ten Commandments:

> "And God spoke all these words: ² 'I am the Lord your God, who brought you out of Egypt, out of the land of slavery.'" (Exodus 20:1-2)

He was in essence saying, "I already am your personal, loving God, and I already did what you so badly needed me to do: deliver you from your enemies.

"So, since I have already established that I am for you, and with you, and always out before you, what I am about to say, these commandments, are for you, for your best interests, for you to live the A+ Life that is truly life."

Then, as he proceeds to the 4th Sabbath commandment, he reminds the Israelites of his gift of the Sabbath.

In Deuteronomy 5, forty years after first hearing and receiving the Ten Commandments, the people surely needed to be reminded of the preeminence of God's Sabbath commandment to keep the Sabbath holy. But they also needed to be reminded of who and what they were before God so graciously saved them: slaves.

And so do we.

Because so were we.

Slaves.

The Israelites were slaves to their Egyptian masters. You and I are slaves to our own Self-ordained masters. Here are just a few:

Work
Self
Fear – Worry – Anxiety
Feelings
What others think
Self-doubt
Control
"If I don't, it won't"
Success
Happiness

You can fill in your own masters, if you are willing to be honest and objective. And of course 'work' is at the top of the list, but perhaps not in the way you might think.

In Egypt the Israelites were slaves with absolutely no value except what they could produce: bricks. Seven days a week, week in and week out, it was all about bricks. Not enough bricks in the eyes of their masters? No value.

Now stop and take a deep breath, because here comes a high beam floodlight, the essence of this entire Sabbath journey:

You are no different from the Israelites in Egypt. You find your value in what you can produce. Your master is the culture, and the culture defines your "quota." All the Churchian men I know define themselves by the cultural quota of what they produce. This includes their income level of course, but also their community production, as well as their church activity production. But sadly, this is true for many Christians as well.

If they earn more than their peer group, they can feel good about themselves. If they do not, they cannot. I have encountered many solid Christian men, who love the Lord and trust him implicitly, who still measure themselves by what they earn. I know men with wonderful marriages and wonderful children, something few men actually have, and yet they cannot help but measure their true quota by their income level. The culture demands it!

A great marriage and well-balanced and happy children? Oh, that's nothing compared to making more bricks, I mean... more money.

For other men their quota, what defines them as a success, what gives them value in their eyes, is measured by their community importance. And for others it is their church importance. Of course it could also include material things, such as golf, Harley-Davidsons, hunting, athletic ability, you name it, we men can be defined and measured by it.

For you ladies who work outside the home, your value may be defined just like us knuckle-head men: brick production. And try as you might, if you are also a mother, your value is tied to your children's production ... and how well they are meeting their quotas, especially compared to your friends' children.

It is also no surprise your value is also defined by how you dress, and your community activities, as well as church activities.

You and I are no different than the Israelite slaves: our value is in our quota production. So we must – we must! – keep busy, and work, work, work, to maintain our value. We have to be busy, or else we risk the worst of all possible outcomes: not being thought of as important.

And this we simply cannot tolerate.
God reminds them,

> "And God spoke all these words: 2 'I am the Lord your
> God, who brought you out of Egypt, out of the land of
> slavery.'"

Can't you just hear God saying, "So stop the madness of measuring yourselves by what you produce!"

And he is saying the same thing to you, "Stop the madness of measuring yourself by how busy you are. Take a day to do nothing. You are of infinite value to me, bricks or no bricks."

But isn't this just so hard for us to do?

Your loving Heavenly Father is saying to you, today, "Remember, I loved you first, when you had no brick value to me. You were a sinner, immersed in the slavery of Self. But I have rescued you from that slavery.

> "For he has rescued us from the dominion of darkness
> and brought us into the kingdom of the Son he loves, [14]
> in whom we have redemption, the forgiveness of sins."
> (Colossians 1:13-14)

"You are a human being, not a human doing. Your value is in me, and my immense love and adoration for you. Your value is in being my beloved child. Nothing more, nothing less. So stop all this doing for at least one day, and just be.

"Be my child, safe and secure. The barbarians are at the gate, but my love and my peace will provide a garrison around your heart and your mind, flooding you with the peace of just being. On my day, rest, reflect, rejuvenate, recover and remember who's you are."

Rest, renewal and reverence take time ... still time ... be still time.

Be still and know that I am God. (Psalm 46:10)
Be still and know that I am
Be still and know that I

Be still and know that
Be still and know
Be still and
Be still
Be

REMEMBER THIS!

Before we conclude, I feel compelled to remind you this is no self-help Sabbath journey. You are going to need the power of the Holy Spirit to truly navigate through this journey to God's Kingdom of peace. You must do your part, but you must also tap into the power already within you, that is, if you are saved.

So one final reminder about what truly matters. Are you saved? Have you surrendered your kingdom to the Kingdom of God, and his crown Prince, Jesus?

Are you sure?

Because none of any of this is going to matter if you are still king of your kingdom.

So remember this:

"Now, brothers, I want to **remind** you of the gospel I preached to you, which you received and on which you have taken your stand. ² By this gospel you are saved, if you hold firmly to the word I preached to you. Otherwise, you have believed in vain.

³ For what I received I passed on to you as of first importance: that Christ died for our sins according to the Scriptures, ⁴ that he was buried, that he was raised on the third day according to the Scriptures, ⁵ and that he appeared to Peter, and then to the Twelve. ⁶ After that, he appeared to more than five hundred of the brothers at the same time, most of whom are still living, though some have fallen asleep.

[7] Then he appeared to James, then to all the apostles, [8] and last of all he appeared to me also, as to one abnormally born. [9] For I am the least of the apostles and do not even deserve to be called an apostle, because I persecuted the church of God." (1 Corinthians 15:1-9 bold added)

Remember, Jesus died so he could rescue you from your own self-imprisoned slavery. It's the only way to his salvation. It is the only way to his Love, joy, peace, patience ...." (Galatians 5:22)

Remember, this is no self-help religion. It is a living, moving, growing, empowering relationship with the Savior of the world, Jesus the Christ, without whom, you do not stand a chance. Without whom, you will always be a slave to your *Self*, and therefore to Satan, and you will miss the "A+ lift that is truly life."

So ... remember, God invites you to, "Be still and know that I am God," by resting on his Sabbath.

Remember, Jesus invites you, as Eugene Peterson states,

"Learn the unforced rhythms of grace."

You can, you know. You can learn these unforced rhythms of God's creating and restoring. You can learn these unforced rhythms of being, not doing. You can learn to take a day to rest, reflect, play ... *unforced* ... whatever feeds your soul, and feeds the Spirit inside you. You can learn to Sabbath.

This beautiful rhythm is inside you. You can find it.

May you not be so caught up in doing, in producing your quotas, that you miss simply being. And may you begin your own personal Sabbath journey to find this kingdom of freedom from the slavery of always doing.

EPILOGUE

A SABBATH JOURNEY RECAP

S A RECAP, I'D LIKE TO COVER A FEW OF MY, "IF YOU MISS everything else, don't miss this" observations.

To – From: Is whatever you are considering doing on your Sabbath going to draw you to the Lord or from the Lord? This is far more important than, "Is this okay to do on Sunday?" During my Sabbath exploration, I have found some things naturally draw me towards the Lord, and others away from him.

We're not talking about going to church versus going to a strip club, but instead about weighing out options of good activities versus better/best activities. A walk in beautiful and lively downtown Greenville is nice, but a quiet walk in the woods drew me closer *to* the Lord.

The Sabbath is not about, "Can I do this?" but, "Is there something better I could be doing?" Something perhaps that will draw you closer to your Lord, to your spouse, to your children?

Isaiah 58:13-14 Do not "Do as you please."

No to-do List: So not accomplish anything on this list.

Set Apart: Holy means to "set apart," so I looked for ways to set my Sundays apart. Little things, like lighting a candle on Sunday morning, not wearing a watch, sitting in a different room to spend my early morning with the Lord. Monday – Saturday I drink my Chinese super-duper antioxidant "Pu-erh" tea, which is so healthy it is void of all taste, unless you think dirt has a taste. But on Sundays I indulge in my instant cappuccino.

These little things help remind me this is a different day, and I want to be mindful it is the Lord's Day, not mine.

Not Mine: Self is my #1 combatant. I need to be reminded often I am not God, and I've found no quicker reminder than seeking to keep the Sabbath holy. Sadly, I want my way, all the time. But now, at least one day a week, I am letting God have his way with my ... oops ... his day.

Lighten Up – Tighten Up: Jesus used the Sabbath, with all its minutia of Jewish restrictions, to deliver his favorite message: "You people have tightened up in all the wrong places - your performance - and have lightened up where it matters most, your hearts.

We have tightened up our performance so no one can criticize our behavior, but we are loosy-goosy in our hearts, where it counts the most, allowing a vast variety of negative thoughts and emotions.

Garrison: The Barbarians of our noisy, frenetic and intrusive culture are at the gate and they are never turning back. But the Sabbath can be the foundation of the garrison God will help you build to guard against these invasions.

A day set apart to the Lord, from your everyday pressing and stressing, can serve to provide a garrison for you, from all the electronic intrusions, busyness and clutter, and even against those inner voices crying out: "Do something! Accomplish something! For crying out loud, you can't just relax all day."

But you can. God knows you need to, so he commanded you to do so.

Rhythms: Everything about our existence, our universe, yes even our bodies, is designed by God with a rhythm in mind. I am learning to bring the Sabbath into my life as a way of getting into his rhythm, and as I have, I see how this permeates the other six days, creating a more harmonious flow, rather than a herky-jerky, reacting approach to life.

Conclusion: The Sabbath commandant is one of the most repeated commandments in all of scripture – by far. What I have learned about the Lord is anything so important to him, is only so important *to* him, because he knows how important it is *for* us.

One thing is for sure, the Sabbath is much bigger than just a day to rest, and it is far beyond just what we should and should not do that day. God intends for his Sabbath to transform your life. How, I'd not sure. But I am sure he is sure.

So rest in this knowledge that he loves you perfectly, and knows exactly what you need to flourish and thrive. You need his rest, and you need his rhythm.

You need his Sabbath.

Remember, this is war.

APPENDIX A

WHY YOUR CHILDREN NEED THE SABBATH

---

by Jen Wilkin
Provided by THEGOSPELCOALITION
Used with permission

M Y OLDEST SON STARTED HIGH SCHOOL THIS FALL. AT his orientation, the counselors spoke to parents about the greatest challenge they see students face in school.

I expected to hear about poor study habits or substance abuse, but to my initial surprise, these were not at the top of the list. Apparently, the greatest challenge presenting itself in the office of the high school guidance counselor is a growing number of kids struggling with anxiety and depression.

Can you guess why?

A combination of overscheduling and sleep deprivation, linked to two main contributors: electronics use and extracurricular activities. We were encouraged as parents to go home and talk to our teenagers about setting boundaries in these areas. Parents across the auditorium scribbled notes furiously as the counselors outlined some suggestions: limit texting, monitor bedtimes, cut back on team practices. I couldn't help but think to myself: *Tonight there will be many demonstrations of teenage angst when Mom shows up with her new list of suggestions.*

What is unfolding at my son's high school is a clear illustration of spiritual truth: the need for regular periods of rest in our lives.

From the earliest pages of the Bible, we find God instituting patterns of activity and rest — not just any kind of rest, but rest with the intent to engage in worship and community. The concept of Sabbath weaves its way through the Old Testament and the New, occupying a prominent place among the Ten Commandments and informing our understanding of heaven.

Despite biblical precedent, few Christians understand or practice Sabbath as a regular part of life, and, consequently, neither do their children.

Christian parents bear the responsibility of teaching our children the value of rest, through our words and through our actions. Children don't set the calendar in our homes — if they are overscheduled or sleep deprived, the fault lies with us. How can we better discharge our duty of raising children to seek Sabbath? To value downtime to reconnect with God and family?

While I admire the high school guidance counselors' optimism, age 14 is probably too late to start imposing boundaries on our child's rest habits and schedule. We need a plan, and we need it early. How will we safeguard for our families the key Sabbath concepts of rest, worship and community?

Here are a few suggestions that have helped our family to honor God in our rest.

ELECTRONICS.

Late-night texting and TV watching, online chatting, surfing the Internet — all can rob a child of rest.

Children between the ages of seven and 12 require a whopping 10 to 11 hours of sleep each night. This is the very age range during which most acquire the electronics to rob them of needed sleep.

Parents can guard their children's rest simply by keeping electronics in sight. We made a rule in our home that no electronics are allowed upstairs: no TVs, computers, phones or games in bedrooms or rooms where their use cannot be monitored.

Each night, those of us who have phones leave them in a spot on the kitchen counter. These measures give us accountability to each other, keep electronics as a shared rather than individual privilege, and force our electronics to obey our family's Sabbath priorities of rest, worship and community.

Well-rested kids bypass many of the unsavory habits of their tired counterparts: fits, backtalk, forgetfulness, drama, isolation and, yes, anxiety and depression. Guarding your child's rest actually gives him or her a running start at Christlike behavior, even during adolescence.

ACTIVITIES.

So many to pursue, so little time. Don't be fooled: The proliferation of activity options for children reflects our cultural affluence, not our child's need to be well rounded or socialized.

Gobs of money are being made off of our misplaced desire to expose our kids to every possible talent path. How can we choose activities for our family in a way that doesn't compromise Sabbath principles?

Because the four Wilkin kids are close in age, our schedule and finances forced us to limit activities to "one or none" for each child. Not all families need to impose a limit this low, but we have re-learned something our grandparents probably knew: Children who participate in no organized activities at all still lead lives full of activity and joy.

To many parents, the idea of a child on no sports team, in no music lessons, at no club meetings is completely foreign and a little frightening. Won't they get bored? Won't they drive me crazy lurking around the house? Won't they miss out on an NFL career and blame me? Or, my personal favorite: Won't other parents think I'm a bad parent?

I would answer all of these questions, "Maybe, but who cares?"

As is often lamented, parenting is not a popularity contest. With that in mind, here are some good (and highly unpopular) questions to ask when evaluating which activity to pursue:

1. Does it sabotage weekend downtime or worship?
2. Does it sabotage family dinners?
3. Does it sabotage bedtime?
4. Does it pull our family apart or push us together?
5. Is it an activity my child can enjoy/benefit from into adulthood?
6. Can we afford it?

Notice that, "Does my child enjoy it?" is not on the list.

So often, I hear parents justify keeping a child in a time-sucking activity because, "He loves it *so much*." Kids love Skittles and Mario Kart *so much*, but they don't get to decide if, when and how much to consume. Because children possess a limited range of life experience, it is difficult for them to conceive of happiness outside their current circumstance. It is our job to help them learn.

LESS THAN ADMIRABLE MOTIVES.

Why do we have such a hard time as parents placing limits on electronics and activities?

Both can appeal to parents for less than admirable reasons. Both can serve as a babysitter or a diversion.

But the appeal of activities extends even farther, to our very identity as parents. We actually want to be labeled "soccer mom" on rhinestone-studded tee shirts and coffee mugs. We carefully arrange our car decals so every identity marker is announced. The thought of removing or withholding our child from an activity threatens the very way we view ourselves.

Maybe our view needs to adjust to something a bit higher. Families that prioritize Sabbath fix their eyes on, and find their identity in, Christ, recognizing their greatest potential for missed opportunity lies not in neglecting activities, but in neglecting time — lots of it — spent together as a family in worship, rest and community with each other.

God forbid we value the discipline of a sport more than the discipline of Christian living.

Both require great application of time and effort, but one is worth far more than the other. Because time is our most limited resource, how we allocate it reveals much about our hearts.

Our time usage should look radically different than that of the unbelieving family. We must leave time for slow afternoons, for evening meals where we pray together and share our faith and struggles, for Sunday mornings of shared worship.

God ordains Sabbath for our good and for his glory. May our homes be places where Sabbath rest is jealously guarded, that in all things God might have pre-eminence — even our schedules.

> **Ephesians 5:15-17**: See then that you walk circumspectly, not as fools but as wise, redeeming the time, because the days are evil. Therefore do not be unwise, but understand what the will of the Lord is.

Made in the USA
Middletown, DE
21 November 2023

43124485R00078